Advance Praise
for
Canada's BEST CAREERS Guide

- *Frank Feather's powerful vision and consistently positive view is unique. Tantalizing and challenging, this effective career planning tool will be valuable to anyone hoping to build a successful career.*
  —Janis Foord Kirk, Careers Columnist, **The Toronto Star.**

- *A great source of inspiration, this book conveys a realistic picture of the changing world and projects you into the future. Its analysis of the changing workforce is of great value for anyone planning their professional life.*
  —Jeannine Renaud, Co-author, *Careers Orientation & Planning,* Independent Learning Centre, **Ontario Ministry of Education.**

- *Germane and extremely valuable as a counselling tool.*
  —Counsellor, **Employment & Immigration Canada**, Winnipeg.

- *A uniquely Canadian effort at forecasting job opportunities by Canada's foremost authority on the future.*
  —**Career Information Resource Advisory Group**, Montréal.

- *Very well written and practical.*
  —**Vocational Psychologist**, Red Deer, Alberta.

- *Fantastic book!*
  —**Communications Consultant**, Surrey, BC.

- *Exceptionally well written and informative.*
  —Coordinator, **Stay in School Program**, Winnipeg.

- *We have a hard time keeping it on the shelf.*
  —**Librarian**, Halifax.

- *Must reading for our whole family.*
  —**Parent**, Etobicoke, Ontario.

- *Just the book I've been looking for.*
  —**High-School Student**, Edmonton.

D0316855

Canada's
BEST
CAREERS
Guide

FRANK FEATHER

Warwick Publishing Inc.
Toronto   Los Angeles

Canada's BEST CAREERS Guide
Copyright © 1987, © 1990, © 1994 by Frank Feather

Publishing History:
1st Edition 1987 (Global Management Bureau)
2nd Edition 1990 (Global Management Bureau)
3rd Edition 1994 (Warwick Publishing/Firefly Books)

Publisher: Warwick Publishing,
 24 Mercer Street, Suite 200, Toronto, Ontario, M5V 1H3

Distributor: Firefly Books Ltd.,
 250 Sparks Avenue, Willowdale, Ontario, M2H 2S4

Jacket design: Nick Pitt

ISBN: 1-895629-30-6

Printed and bound in Canada

Contents

SECTION B:
Industry-by-Industry Career Prospect Review 37

SECTION E:
Lifelong Learning for Career Success 117

CONCLUSION:
Envisioning Your Future Success 127

Preface

HELP WANTED
2.8 Million Canadians

Canada is looking for 2.8 million creative hard-
working people for rewarding careers in healthcare,
information management, and leisure marketing.
(Note: Farmers, assembly-line workers, and
switchboard operators need not apply.)

If Canadian employers took out a collective help-wanted ad for
the next decade, that's what it might say. Canadian employment will increase by a robust 1.5% a year between 1994 and
2005.

With all those jobs to be filled, how come we have so many
Canadians out of work?

I first explained this in an article "Switch from Manufacturing to Service Economy Could Affect Careers" in the *Career
Campus Directory* of 1977. In part, I wrote:

*As Canada enters the "Post-Industrial" revolution ... this
poses serious questions:*
- *Are people really being trained for future jobs or for
  work that's going the way of dinosaurs?*
- *What are schools and universities doing to gear
  students to new job trends?*
- *Do displaced workers know where to go to get
  counselling to train for new kinds of work?*
- *What are the best careers of tomorrow?"*

The answer to the first three questions is still to be found in the chronic youth unemployment statistics—17 years later!

Responsibility for this neglect can only be laid at the doorstep of short-sighted politicians and government bureaucrats who don't understand the future into which they are supposed to be leading us.

Why *JOB FUTURES* is Seriously Flawed
The Ministry of Employment (Unemployment?) publishes *JOB FUTURES*. But this "occupational outlook" guide has a dismal track record. For example, the 1985 edition said the best job growth to 1992 would occur in three job groups: secretaries/stenos (being replaced by wordprocessors), bookkeepers (being automated out of existence), and truck drivers (despite the decline of the manufacturing sector). The 1987 edition was no better, again saying the best job growth would be for bookkeepers, secretaries/stenos, and (this time) farmers, even though the farm economy was in worse shape than the 1930s.

The federal computer was more alarmingly off the mark in terms of percentage growth rates. The fastest-growing job category (at 53%) was funeral directors! And, while Canada long-ago moved from an agricultural/industrial economy to one based on services, the government insisted that we needed more farmers and truck drivers. *JOB FUTURES* is so absurd that employment in every single job category is forecast to increase. This defies the logic that certain jobs simply die out.

So much for official Government of Canada job forecasts. They clearly ignore future trends in society, technology or the economy at large. *JOB FUTURES* is a dangerously misleading publication that could direct you to a dead-end career!

Pointing Canadians Towards Career Success
All other books on future jobs are American and, in most cases, show an incomplete or faulty understanding of the changing economy and its impact on future career prospects.

Consequently, Canadian students are frequently being mis-educated for tomorrow's job needs and are not being directed (by all governments, many parents, some teachers, and even a few counsellors) into fields where there is the greatest demand. My experience in giving 300+ speeches to more than 80,000 Canadian educators and students about the future makes it clear that there is a fuzzy understanding of the changing job market or where the best career paths are.

Yet, as I shall describe, the late-1990s and early part of the 21st century will witness an economic "Super-Boom." As individuals and as a nation we must be ready to take advantage of the coming period of prosperity. My hope is that this book will help refocus the career paths of Canada's future workforce to take advantage of this unrivaled opportunity.

That's why I first wrote *Canada's BEST CAREERS Guide* and that's why I've completely revised, expanded and updated this new 1994 edition.

Who Will Benefit From This Book?
The earlier editions of this book received a positive response from a wide audience. Based on reader feedback, this updated version will be of use to students, guidance counsellors, parents, educators and librarians—to all those involved in career planning and guidance—as follows:

For Students
• Explains what's ahead, identifies the best jobs, and helps you pick the career most suited to your personality;
• Makes career planning easy, guiding you with hands-on worksheets, charts, and dozens of jobs lists.

For Guidance Counsellors
• Simplifies your job with fresh, effective, "future relevant" approaches;
• Lets you give clients accurate, up-to-date, easy-to-use, and uniquely Canadian career information.

For Parents
● Helps you solve your child's career worries; guides him/her into a lasting career, not just any old job;
● Lets you to invest in your child's future—and maybe your own!

For Educators
● Helps you tailor the curriculum to future career needs.

For Librarians
● Provides high-interest Canadian material that virtually guarantees popularity and heavy circulation.

Dazzling Career Opportunities
To those who are alert, career prospects in the late-1990s and into the 21st century are dazzling! Never before have there been so many different job and career opportunities; an enormous variety of fascinating options for you to choose from. To help you find tomorrow's best careers, the book has 5 sections:

Section A: "Big Picture" Overview of Dynamics of Change
The first essential in planning a successful career is an understanding of how the world is changing; of how future trends are transforming the Canadian economy and, hence, the job market. Section A discusses the future in broad detail, painting a "big picture" of the trends that will have the greatest impact on Canada's job market during the next ten years.

Section B: Industry-by-Industry Career Prospects Review
The second key is to understand how the broad trends reshaping the economy will impact on specific Canadian industries. Section B reviews the major jobs that will decline or become obsolete and alerts you to new jobs that are emerging or will expand strongly. The best jobs are listed for each sector.

Section C: Best Careers Ranked Forecasts for 1995-2005

To help you identify the best career opportunities across the entire Canadian economy, regardless of sector, Section C provides rankings of the best, the average, and the worst career prospects. These tables provide forecasts of growth to the year 2005 in some 200 jobs.

Section D: Futuristic Career Planning with Worksheets

Before embarking on a career path, you also need to plan that career. The best career will be one that is most suitable to you and your desired future lifestyle. Section D helps you get a fix on your future life and on your own personality so that you can select the best job that is most suitable for you. That way, you'll be the most happy and successful.

Section E: Lifelong Learning for Career Success

Finally, and most important, you must be suitably educated for your chosen career. Gone are the days when a High School Diploma would last you a lifetime. Advanced education and a variety of other skills are the keys to the future. Extra qualifications and skills upgrading will become a career-long pursuit. Without such competence, the best careers simply will not be available to you in the 21st century. This section discusses the skills base you will need.

To get the most out of this book, please read each Section in turn. Let's start with the "big picture" of the Canada's future.

Section A

"Big Picture" Overview of the Dynamics of Change

Which jobs really offer the best opportunities to leap ahead?

Before we can answer that question, we must understand how society at large is changing. Future career success starts with knowledge about the future in general. To recognize where tomorrow's best jobs or careers will be, it is necessary to understand what the future of Canada will look like. To unravel *that* puzzle, we must analyze the forces of change that are shaping the immediate future. These forces range from global to national to provincial, and involve social, technical, economic and political dynamics.

If Canada were a closed society and never changed, this analysis would be fairly easy because, in the end, each of us is the servant of everybody else—in one way or another, either directly or indirectly, either totally or in part. Therefore if you look around today's society, noting down all the needs and wants of all the citizens, you would soon develop a list of all the jobs which have to be done if those needs and wants are to be met for everyone.

Of course, nothing is quite that simple. The world—and Canada—changes constantly. People age and their needs and wants change. New people are born with their own unique set of needs. Technology also changes society directly and indirectly, changing or replacing old jobs and creating new ones.

Also, of course, Canada is *not* a closed society. We are open to the world. In the new global economy, no country can isolate or insulate itself from the external trade and technology.

Each nation is now a "province" of the world. Canadian workers are now part of the global labour pool, and jobs will be performed where the global market dictates.

6-Wave Restructuring of Canada's Economy

To understand Canada's future, it is therefore important to study some basic revolutionary shifts in the global economy.

In his book *The Third Wave*, Alvin Toffler identified the onset of "third wave" post-industrial society. The "first" and "second" waves were the agricultural and industrial economies respectively. Figure 1 shows the shift of employment between the 1st-, 2nd- and 3rd-Waves in various groups of countries between 1960 and 1980 with a forecast to the year 2000.

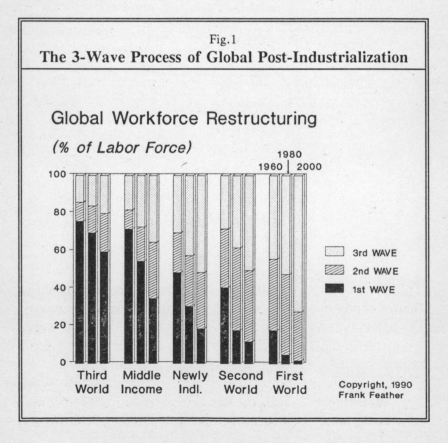

Fig.1
The 3-Wave Process of Global Post-Industrialization

Global Workforce Restructuring

(% of Labor Force)

Copyright, 1990
Frank Feather

In developing countries, which are mostly crop-growing societies, people still work on a labour-intensive basis, just as people in Canada did in the Agricultural Age. But, as in Canada before them, these countries are experiencing a continual shift of employment from the labour-intensive farming sector to the industrial and service sectors as their economies modernizes. As machines take over agricultural tasks, the rural population moves to the cities, where they form industrial labour pools for the manufacturing and service sectors.

In Canada, this process has gone the farthest. A century ago, agriculture alone employed 80% of Canadians; today it employs only 3%. Jobs moved from the farm to the factory. Since 1950 or so, we have been moving jobs from the factory to the office; to the post-industrial or service sector of the economy. Today, about 80% of Canadians work in the "third wave" post-industrial sector.

Indeed, the "third wave" sector is now so large it must be broken down into smaller parts in order to understand it. In reality, Canada now has a 6-wave economy *(see Figure 2, overleaf)* as follows:

- 1st-Wave: Agriculture/Natural Resources/Energy
- 2nd-Wave: Industry/Manufacturing/Robotics
- 3rd-Wave: Financial/Healthcare/Personal Services
- 4th-Wave: Information/Knowledge/High-Technology
- 5th-Wave: Leisure & Tourism
- 6th-Wave: Outer-Space Economy

These waves exist simultaneously in each Canadian province, though at any one time, one wave prevales. In some provinces, the 1st-Wave Agriculture sector is stronger than elsewhere. Conversely, the 1st-Wave doesn't exist at all in Metro Toronto where the 3rd, 4th, and 5th Waves are the strongest.

The old waves rarely disappear; rather, the new waves complement them. Thus, machines built in the 2nd-Wave manufacturing sector helped modernize 1st-Wave agriculture and

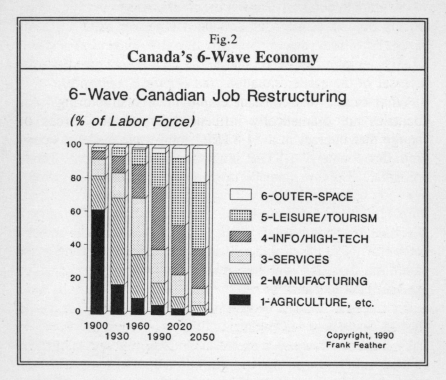

Fig.2
Canada's 6-Wave Economy

6-Wave Canadian Job Restructuring

(% of Labor Force)

6-OUTER-SPACE
5-LEISURE/TOURISM
4-INFO/HIGH-TECH
3-SERVICES
2-MANUFACTURING
1-AGRICULTURE, etc.

1900 1960 2020
   1930 1990 2050

Copyright, 1990
Frank Feather

increased crop production. Today, the 4th-Wave information sector is not just spawning the information economy, it is helping to modernize all other sectors of the economy. Computerized information is essential to modern economic activity, be it on a farm or at a factory, office, hospital, or hotel.

In Canada as a whole, the 3rd-Wave service sector became the largest employer in 1950. This was the real 3rd-Wave revolution. The next wave, the 4th-Wave Information sector (of computers, information, and knowledge professions) began to rise to supremacy in the 1980s. As of 1994, this wave is the main job creator in Canada. However, the fastest-growing employment area is the 5th-Wave Leisure sector, that is, the travel, tourism, hospitality, recreation, entertainment and cultural industry. Looking further ahead to the future, the 6th-Wave of Outer-Space is emerging as a new employment sector.

I'll say much more about these waves in Section B.

"4-STEP" Process of Employment Restructuring

During the last century, as Canada has moved from an farm-based 1st-Wave society through to a 4th-Wave Information society, employment has shifted to an almost upside-down reversal of the earlier situation *(see Figure 2, opposite)*.

What causes this constant employment restructuring? All countries are dramatically influenced by various forces of change that interact in a "4-STEP" long-wave cycle of economic development. 4-STEP is my acronym for Social, Technological, Economic and Political change, as follows:

Step 1: Social Motivation

Socially, as I said earlier, each of us is the servant of everybody else. Note down society's future needs and you get a list of all the jobs that will be needed. In an aging society, for example, the demand for healthcare workers will soar beyond today's needs. And, as people age, their other needs also will change. Eldercare will replace childcare as a primary focus of Baby Boomers because they all have aging relatives and their children soon will be grown up. As well, new generations of people will be born with their own unique set of needs and new waves of immigrants will bring yet more needs.

Step 2: Technological Innovation

Technology also changes workforce demands. It changes or replaces old jobs and creates new ones. As automobiles and telephones showed, technology also changes how society is structured and functions. Through the "ripple effect" of these innovations, technology indirectly restructures the job market. For example, people made automatic washing machines (instead of wringer-washers and scrubbing boards), micro-wave ovens (instead of convection stoves), and personal computers and word processors (instead of typewriters). In turn, this restructures all jobs in the production-consumption chain—from raw material extraction and fabrication to marketing, sales, and the use of these products.

Step 3: Economic Modernization

Economically, in the *Global Village* every nation is a province of the world. Workers are now part of a global labor pool and work will be done where the market dictates. Global information flows bring new ideas, new values, new needs and wants. This creates demand for new products and services—and new jobs to deliver them. New ideas of production (such as robots and computers) and new consumer products (such as VCRs, microwave ovens, personal computers, FAX machines, or ethnic foods) create new markets—and a host of yet more new jobs in serving the needs of a diversified market.

Step 4: Political Reformation

The major political dynamic is the environmental concern, globally and locally, from worries about the ozone layer to problems of local garbage disposal. Indeed, the environment is now a major element of every sector and a major industry itself.

This 4-STEP cycle of change is completely re-inventing Canada and restructuring the workforce.

Future Growth in the Post-Industrial Workforce

Clearly, as the second bar chart shows, most future job growth will occur in the post-industrial sectors of the economy, particularly in the 3rd-, 4th-, and 5th-Wave sectors.

• **3rd-Wave:** Everything we do, from morning to night, is made possible by workers in the 3rd-wave service economy—in a bank, doctor's office, dry cleaning, or other service outlet. This sector will continue to provide jobs galore. During the next decade, 10% of new jobs will be health-related and many of the fastest-growing jobs fields are indirectly related to healthcare.

• **4th-Wave:** Without doubt, the information/knowledge and high-tech sector is the wave of the short-term future.

A new computer goes into use every two seconds. They will be carried in briefcases, pockets, and purses by everyone. Closely related with computers is the telecom industry. In a global economy, the effective management of information flows is vital, and entirely new industries are being spawned around this dynamic. Biotechnology (biotech) could also transform dozens of other industries, from farming and mining to pharmaceuticals and pollution control. Biotech could even rival computers in job creation within the next 20 years.

- **5th-Wave:** Thanks to tele-computers, we are succeeding magnificently at putting ourselves out of work. The leisure industry already provides 20% of all jobs and hospitality will be the growth industry of the next 30 years. Since the recession of the early-1990s, the industry has resumed its fast-track growth, creating thousands of jobs. Arts, culture, and sports are now a major leisure activity, with galleries, museums, orchestras, and theatres starting up across the continent—and creating a multitude of jobs.

Expanding on this brief overview, the rest of this section explains the future of the Canada and its job market between now and 2005.

The 4-STEP Canadian Future:
What it Will Be Like in the Year 2005

Simply stated, the 1990s are changing our lives more than any decade before. In the early-1990s, many people experienced job dislocation. But most people will find the late-1990s a time of liberation, of greater freedom, and prosperous career opportunities. They will feel at ease with the future and in control of their own destiny as we move into the 21st century.

We Create Our Own Future
It is important to realize that the future is not something impersonal, imposed upon us from "somewhere out there" by mysterious forces. We create our own future. As we search for clues to identify technological, economic and political trends, we find that everything always starts with people.

Technology is not thrust upon us; it is people who create new scientific breakthroughs and technical applications. People cause pollution—and decide to clean it up. No matter how strong the seduction of people-created advertising, people decide how much they'll spend/borrow or save/ invest to satisfy their economic needs and aspirations. People create bureaucracy and break through it. People elect politicians—and then decide to replace them with genuine leaders.

In short, human behaviour creates social, technical, economic and political change. Let's review, then, the 4-STEP future of Canada, starting with the social dynamics of change that will affect career prospects.

Social ("High-Touch") Dynamics of Change
Every society literally regenerates itself with each new generation of people. Five major social dynamics are changing the Canadian job market. I call these the "high-touch" dynamics

because they require all of us to be sensitive to the changing needs and aspirations of the new Canadian population.

1. Multicultural or Polyglot Society

The Canadian population will grow to 32-million plus by the year 2005. However, because the birth rate is not high enough to replace our population on an ongoing basis, almost all of this growth will come from immigration. While newcomers increase the competition for available jobs, they actually create more jobs than they take. This is because they need all kinds of goods and services, from houses to clothing, food, household appliances, financial services, leisure activities, etc. Immigration will therefore continue to expand the population and, hence, the career market dramatically.

Immigration also is changing the make-up of Canada's population. The vast majority of Canadian immigrants used to come from Europe. While some still come from there, since the mid-1980s about 80% of immigrants have come from Asia and developing countries. This trend will continue, changing Canada from a nation of mostly Europeans to a global-polyglot or truly multicultural society.

This influx of new immigrants from other parts of the world is bringing new values and new demands for different kinds of products and services—all of which have to be marketed and sold in new ways. For example, clothes fashions will change and multicultural restaurants of all kinds will continue to dot the Canadian landscape.

Most immigrants also will continue to settle in major urban centres, particularly Toronto and Vancouver, creating continued economic growth and, hence, job demand in those centres.

2. Middle-Aging and Aging Society

Another aspect of population growth stems from the aging of Canada's existing population. People are simply living longer. Thanks to the miracles of modern medicine and an emphasis on improved lifestyles and physical fitness, there will be tens of thousands of people in the year 2000 who will be 80-, 90- and over 100-years-old. There will be more people 65-years-old or older than there will be 18-years-old or younger, creating a potential labour shortage in some fields and driving up wages and salaries.

Since people are living longer and healthier lives, they will continue to create a demand for products and services which, in turn, will fuel yet more job demand. At the same time, despite their improved health, people in their declining years will require all kinds of care such as in-home help, shopping services and healthcare.

The most important demographic shift in Canada in the 1990s, however, is not so much the aging but the *middle*-aging of Canadian society. One third of the Canadian population is accounted for by the Baby Boom generation (those born between 1946 and 1964) who, by the year 2005, will be between 40- and 60-years-old.

Having formed their families and established their homes, their attention now is on educating their children and improving the quality of their life. Their overall emphasis will be on leisure, the arts, culture, more relaxing forms of recreation (such as golf instead of jogging), and further education. With large amounts of disposable income, this generation of Canadians will create a huge demand for jobs in the new waves of the economy.

3. Women Achieving Equal Power with Men

Women are also changing Canadian society in dramatic ways. I used to make what many people thought was a rash prediction that 50% of all the top jobs in Canada by the year 2000 would be held by women. Well, each day brings this prediction closer to reality.

The women's movement is a natural part of post-industrialism. The shift from labour-intensive 1st-Wave agriculture and 2nd-Wave manufacturing to 3rd-Wave services activity changed the family structure so there was less need for child-bearing.

This allowed women to gain access to higher education, which in turn equipped them with the ability to leave the home to develop careers and become financially independent of a male "bread winner." Large numbers of women are now moving into the corridors of power: in business, the professions and politics.

The business graduates who tomorrow will be running most of Canada's corporations graduated from college in the 1980s and early-1990s. More than half of them were women. In fact, 1985 marked the first year that Canadian graduate business schools enrolled more females than males.

As these graduates move into male-dominated institutions they are working together as change agents to modify the predominant macho, 2nd-Wave industrial pattern of Canadian organizational behaviour.

This will emerge more strongly as they reach higher levels of decision-making in the late-1990s. Beyond the year 2000, I'm confident both sexes will be able to develop their careers and manage their organizations in environments free of sex-role constraints.

In the professions, in 1992 women earned 61% of the bachelor degrees, 52% of the masters degrees, and 34% of the doctoral degrees awarded in Canada. As a result, women have made substantial inroads into what have been traditionally male-dominated professions. By the year 2000, more women than men will have degrees, guaranteeing them at least equal access to the best careers in the country.

Clearly, tomorrow's best careers are open equally to women and men. Indeed, women now account for 60% of new job entrants and, by the year 2005, 53% of all Canadian workers will be women, up from only 32% in 1972.

Moreover, women also are catching up with men in earnings. Women's salaries have grown from 61% of men's in 1960 to 76% in 1993. The figure will be 90% or more by the year 2005, if not sooner.

4. Healthcare Dynamics

Modern parents are having fewer children. (About 20% are having none at all.) As these children work their way through school, the social emphasis will switch away from the 1980s' concern about childcare. The latest concern is eldercare—the need to look after aging relatives: parents, step-parents, uncles, aunts, grandparents and great-grandparents. The career market will switch in parallel, with far more jobs being created in eldercare than childcare.

An emphasis on health and fitness spread across all segments of society in the 1980s. While middle-age will bring a thickening of waist lines, the aging population will not lose its concern about health and fitness. As discussed at length later, healthcare, fitness and recreation will be the boom industries of the late-1990s and beyond. As people age, they try to retain their overall appearance, their youthfulness and their beauty. Clinics and spas of all kinds will open to cater to their needs.

5. Leisure and Lifestyle Dynamics

The overall desire of human beings is to achieve a leisurely lifestyle. A leisure society is one in which non-physical labour becomes the main human activity and where leisure dominates the economy in terms of employment and output. Wealth mainly stems from the use of intellectual (not so much physical) energy to create technological innovations that are more productive and so make life physically and economically easier.

We constantly use brains over brawn to overcome hardship, improve efficiency, generate wealth and get rid of unpleasant, mundane, laborious tasks. As we make progress, we change our values and attitudes about work. When people are concerned about basic needs, any job will do. The better off they become, however, the better and more secure the job they need to keep their improved economic standing.

Above a certain income level, basic needs are easily met and increased income tends to be surplus. This creates a need for personal achievement and fulfillment that meaningful and stimulating "work" (not necessarily a job) might bring. Most people aspire to work fewer hours, in order to have more time for further education, the arts and leisure.

In the 1980s, the Baby Boom generation gained a reputation for greed and materialistic consumption. In the 1990s, however, having formed their own families, they are changing their values. As the 4th-Wave information economy spreads across Canada, people will become less concerned with material survival. Instead, the emphasis will be on higher values concerned with quality (rather than quantity) of life. As the 5th-Wave leisure society also unfolds, a leisure ethic will be becoming evident. Indeed, a 30-hour workweek by the year 2000 will be enough to maintain an improving quality of life.

In the late-1990s, Canadians will spend more and more time either at home (what marketers call "cocooning"), with their PCs and home entertainment centres, or outside enjoying all that the leisure and entertainment sector of the economy has to offer. The impact on job creation will be dramatic.

Technological ("High-Tech") Dynamics of Change

Just as a new generation of people rejuvenates society, a new generation of technology rejuvenates the economy. Six major technological dynamics are reshaping the job market.

1. New Wave of Technological Change

While invention and innovation occur almost daily, major breakthroughs come in periodic bunches or waves *(see chart, overleaf)*.

The 2nd-Wave manufacturing age began with the Industrial Revolution in the late-1800s. It was based on innovations in transportation (crude cars and airplanes) and communications (telegraph and telephone). It gave rise to production-lines and the widespread use of metals to make the various products of industrial society. World War II interrupted progress but also spurred innovations in computing, microwaves and rocketry.

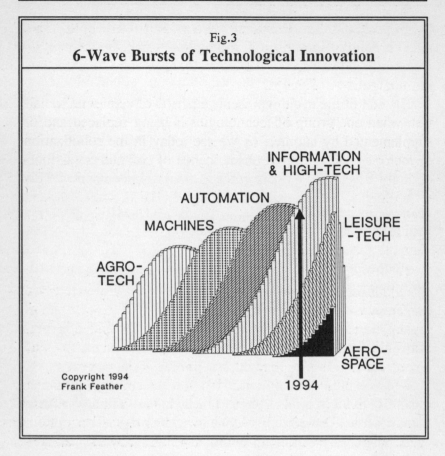

Fig.3
6-Wave Bursts of Technological Innovation

INFORMATION
& HIGH-TECH

AUTOMATION

MACHINES

LEISURE
-TECH

AGRO-
TECH

AERO-
SPACE

Copyright 1994
Frank Feather   1994

In the 1950s and 1960s, new economic growth flowed from these and other inventions. While the automobile came to full economic fruition during this period, the new revolution was driven by new sources of energy (nuclear as well as oil substitutes) and by electronics, mainframe computers and jet airplanes. These innovations spurred the growth of the 3rd-Wave service sector of the economy, creating opportunities in computer manufacturing, which allowed increasing sophistication in the banking and financial services industries.

Technological revolutions thus tend to overlap in a wavelike sequence. Once productive new technologies are fully developed and applied, the economy booms. But solid economic progress does not last for ever. After about 25-years, most technologies peak and their economic benefits start to dwindle. They reach a point of diminishing economic returns; the technology wave turns downward as the technologies wane—or until they are upgraded or replaced.

The end of the cycle represents a period of economic transition when one group of technologies is being replaced and/or supplemented by another, as we see today in the robotization of factories and the rapid obsolescence of computers (as increasingly advanced models replace their predecessors). This technological restructuring obviously displaces some workers in the old sectors of the economy in favour of new jobs in the new sectors.

2. Technology Creates More Jobs than it Replaces

Canada is caught-up in such a painful economic and workplace transition as it finds a new role in a global economy. Technological changes of such magnitude as the electronic revolution—like textile machines of old—cloud the transition and breed fear that more jobs will be eliminated than created.

This is a false fear. It is true that new technology eliminates old jobs, reduces and changes others, and inevitably reduces human work. However, while major technological revolutions cause major disruptions in labour markets, they also create a massive expansion of work in the new sectors of the economy.

Every computer or robot, for example, requires people to design it, to program it, to market it, to deliver and install it, to service it, to operate it—and to develop a newer model to replace it. Such technologies also create thousands of spinoff jobs in companies making parts and supplies such as microchips, electric cables, disk drives, printers, paper and ribbons.

As new technologies replace old tasks, they also enable society to do things that were not before possible. Thus airplanes replaced ocean liners but they carry many more passengers, via an expanding network of international airports, creating yet more jobs in the transport and hotel systems—the supporting infrastructure of the 5th-Wave leisure sector.

3. Technology Reduces Working Hours

As it de-industrializes, Canada is faced with major problems of structural unemployment—especially in certain sectors of the "old" economy. This is a serious but temporary phenomenon. After the Great Depression of the 1930s and the economic re-structuring that followed, the return to economic growth was accompanied by full employment at fewer hours worked. This will again happen during the next 25-years as the world leaves behind the recession of the early-1990s *(discussed later)*.

Part-time employment and shorter working hours will restore full employment, again by sharing work. Unfortunately, only 13% of Canadian firms yet allow people to "share" a job and 60% of companies still persist with the 40-hour workweek.

Instead of sharing work, by reducing the legal work week, since the mid-1980s we have elected to use unemployment insurance as a welfare program to effectively pay 11% of the workforce to stay at home.

Worse yet, this has created one million "forced" unemployed who are missing out on any form of work experience and career development, and their skills are becoming obsolete.

A country that fails to invest in its human resources will not create new real wealth and hence will not prosper. By paying people to stay at home, Canada is failing to invest in its long-term future. In the late-1990s and the early part of the 21st century, Canada will be poorly equipped to take advantage of the new technology-driven boom unless it provides itself with an suitably-trained/educated workforce.

The enormous sums of money now spent on unemployment benefits should be used to give people the chance to prepare themselves for the future labour market. Such money should be paid to Canadian employers as hiring and training incentives. Work experience and education would be gained by those now jobless, who could again become consumers and taxpayers.

This would spur business investment and expand the economy. In turn, the generation of greater wealth would allow working hours to be reduced yet again across the economy.

4. De-Industrialization and Robotization

With manufacturing inevitably shifting to the low-cost sites in developing countries, those Canadian manufacturing entities that survive will be highly automated to achieve optimal levels of efficiency, productivity and quality control. The 2nd-Wave manufacturing age saw mechanical engineering and machine power replace muscle power in the factory. Since about 1970, the factory has been transformed by a new generation of electronic machines in the form of robots and computer systems.

During the 1980s, the number of robots in use worldwide increased from only 50,000 to almost 500,000 and reached 600,000 in 1993. In the late-1990s, robots will become even more common and "flexible manufacturing systems" (that is, fully automated production processes) will eliminate virtually all human labour from Canadian factories. By 2005, robots could be handling all manufacturing chores. In this drive for productivity and efficiency, the one bright career prospect in the 2nd-Wave sector is for roboticists of various types.

5. The Information Superhighway

The world is increasingly encircled by satellites, the "tom-tom drums" of the Global Village. We are living in an electronic world which operates 24-hours/day, 365-days/year. The telecom and computer revolution is the biggest revolution in human history. It will continue to transform our lives and careers in the late-1990s and into the next century.

The next generation of computers will have artificial intelligence capabilities that can translate any language on earth by voice activation. Computers are an extension of the mind and body. The voice box is about to replace the keyboard in computer operations, transforming all jobs everywhere. There will be computers on every desk in every office and school, and in the back of every airplane seat. By the year 2000, 80% of Canadians will have a PC at home. The workplace will be anyplace, creating amazing career opportunities in every sector of the economy.

Meanwhile, expert systems or "know-bots" will issue reports and recommend actions based on data gathered electronically—all without human intervention. By 1993, more than $1-billion had been invested in expert systems by industries such as banking and insurance across North America. While these systems will eliminate many white-collar "number-crunching" jobs, they also will create new business opportunities—and brand new careers.

6. High-Tech Revolution

Other elements of the high-tech revolution are biotechnology, new materials and ceramics, superconductivity, and aerospace research.

Beyond the information superhighway, biotech will be the great technological revolution of the early decades of the 21st century. Biotech integrates biological, physical and chemical sciences in various processes to produce goods. By applying biological techniques to industrial processes, biotech already is creating new products, enhancing the productivity of old industries and helping to protect the environment. We also are using it to develop new industries such as bioelectronics and to modernize traditional 1st-Wave industries such as agriculture, food processing, fishering and forestry.

We're also entering the age of "man-made" materials—the next step in the continuum from Stone Age to Bronze Age to Iron Age. It is based on the creation of composite materials fused from such common elements as clay and sand together with synthetic materials such as plastic and organic compounds. Instead of taking raw materials and forming them into products, science can now identify the products needed and then "compose" them, atom by atom, from whatever materials are required.

Fine ceramics, which are harder and smoother than steel, are increasingly used in car and airplane engines and bodies. The telecom industry is being transformed by microchips made from gallium arsenide, ceramics, and fiber-optic cables made from glass as thin as a human hair—only two of which are needed to handle all trans-Atlantic telephone calls. Healthcare is being transformed by biomaterials (such as artificial tissues, skin, joints, arteries and organs) made from plastics, ceramics, glass, silicon, rubber, carbon, polymers and composite alloys.

The new science of super-conductivity is forcing us to re-think all the ways in which we use electricity. It will revolutionize electronics and transportation, allowing computers to operate at blazing speeds and levitated trains to travel at the speed of sound, all at vastly reduced rates of energy use.

In aerospace research, companies such as General Motors are using space shuttle tests to learn about combustion, pollution control devices and new materials. The 3M Company is pursuing space research to come up with new films, coatings and electronic materials. Weightlessness may allow the creation of purer drugs and the development of fundamentally new medicines. Tests have already been done to produce various substances in quantities 700 times as large (with purity five times as great) as is possible on Earth. Flawless glass, super-strong metal alloys and tough plastics are also potential space lab products.

This is only the tip of the iceberg of experiments in space. With every shuttle flight, something of scientific or business interest is studied and learned. By 2010, space industries could annually produce $65-billion worth of products and services for the 6th-Wave Outer-Space sector of the economy, improving our lives and creating thousands of new jobs in Canada.

Economic ("High-Value") Dynamics of Change

The major dynamics of economic change are all driven by the need to add value to the economy and to expand the economic pie so that we can all become better off.

As these forces come to full fruition in the late-1990s, the impact on the job market will again be dramatic.

1. New Economic Long-Wave Cycle

In parallel with the new waves of technology discussed earlier, there is a long-wave cycle in the economy. This long-wave is typified by an upward and then a downward trend, each lasting 25 to 30 years, and operating like a giant roller-coaster. This is what caused the serious economic disruptions across Canada in the early-1990s.

Where does this long-wave cycle come from? There are various short-term economic cycles, which we call business cycles. These cycles are of various lengths but they all occur together. They compound each other's effects and form an undulating long-wave cycle *(the thick wiggly line in Figure 4)*.

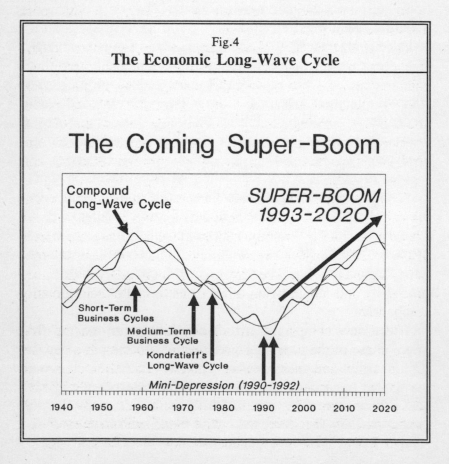

Fig.4
The Economic Long-Wave Cycle

Gross national product (GNP, or the total output value of the economy) suffers severely when the long-wave is at its lowest ebb. This event is usually called a Depression. In reality, the "trough" in the long-wave is marked by two very severe recessions—which I call "Mini-Depressions." One of these, occurring 1981-83, was called the "Great Recession" by economists because it was the worst recession since the 1930s. In 1982, for example, Canada's GNP declined by 4.6% from 1981 and unemployment soared to the highest level since the 1930s.

Canada entered the second "Mini-Depression" in late-1989 and the economy hit bottom in mid-1991. The worst part of the downturn lasted until 1993. Because this "Mini-Depression" occurred at the very bottom of the long-wave, it was more disruptive than that of 1981-83.

The last "Mini-Depression" cleansed the economy of excessive debt, forcing inefficient companies into bankruptcy and encouraging others to replace old technologies with new ones. The old industrial sectors such as fishing, shipping, railroads, and farming suffered greatly while the new sectors of computers and electronics grew rapidly. Unemployment climbed to record levels, particularly in the already struggling sectors and regions of Canada.

With the "Mini-Depression" behind us, there is much room for optimism. Most of the deadwood has been pruned from the Canadian economy and replaced by the shining success stories of the future. We have been building the base of the next economic boom for some time, creating "silicon valleys" of future prosperity and modernizing other firms to make them globally competitive.

These new companies are already taking us into the first boom phase of the next long-wave cycle, ushering in a new set of industries and new wealth creation. The microelectronic revolution in particular is the new engine of economic growth and job creation. The economic take-off will surprise most people and, by the 1996, the entire world will have entered a "Super-Boom" that will extend well into the 21st century.

Information is the new economic commodity. It is the over-whelming source of economic input (raw material) and output (products and services) in all six waves of the economy.

Information-based technologies will be the major source of economic prosperity during the next long-wave cycle and infor-mation oriented jobs will be plentiful everywhere.

2. North American Free Trade Agreement (NAFTA)

During the late-1990s, the gradual elimination of North Amer-ican trade barriers will make Canada part of a much larger economic pie. The increased exposure to U.S. competition, and the logistics of efficient relocation of factories to places closer to the centre of the U.S. market, caused plant closures and severe job loss in Canada during the "Mini-Depression."

But the free access to the huge U.S. market, and the incr-easingly free mobility of labour across the border, will create more than enough jobs to offset the losses as the economy takes off. The addition of Mexico to the free trade pact adds another 90-million consumers to create a huge "AMEXICANA" common market. It follows that many of tomorrow's best Can-adian careers will not be in Canada at all; rather they will be anywhere in "AMEXICANA."

3. Shift from Atlantic to Pacific

The focus on NAFTA has distracted attention from the fact that the centre of gravity of the global economy has shifted from the Atlantic Ocean to the Pacific Ocean. In 1986, the volume of trade across the Pacific exceeded that across the Atlantic for the first time in history. The gap has continued to widen.

The Pacific Rim, led by Japan, is the new powerhouse of the global economy. Canada, of course, is an important Pacific Rim economy and will play a full part in its prosperity. British Columbia in particular will reap significant rewards, leading to much job creation in Western Canada.

4. Shift from North to South

Meanwhile, world manufacturing is constantly moving from the Northern Hemisphere to the Southern Hemisphere, from the developed to the developing countries. The reason for this is a simple matter of economies-of-scale: more than 80% of the world's people live in developing countries; by the year 2005, 90% will live there. The so-called Third World thus represents the future of the world marketplace.

We live on a giant ball, not the flat Earth depicted on a wall map. In a planetary world, it simply does not make sense to extract resources or make products in the North when all the consumers are on the other side of the globe. On the contrary, products are increasingly made more cheaply in the developing countries and shipped back to the developed ones.

We are living on a "planetary production site" and entire industries are on the move. Bata Shoe Limited, the world's largest shoe-making and retailing concern, is a good Canadian example of a company that "looks beyond borders" to become an integral part of the changing global dynamic. Bata runs about 100 factories worldwide from a tiny head office in Toronto, using electronic communications networks to oversee its operations.

If Bata had set up plants all the way across Canada to make shoes for export to the rest of the world, the company today would probably be bankrupt, because it would not have been able to compete with the low production costs that exist in the South. Instead, Bata realized, four decades ago, that it had to set up plants in local markets. The company now has captured about 35% of the world's shoe market and generates wealth in Canada as well as abroad. Indeed, by helping build up foreign economies, those countries are more able to buy *other* things from Canada.

The world clearly is in process of redeciding who is going to make what, and where. This is restructuring the job market, causing Canada's natural resource and manufacturing sectors to lose world market share—and jobs. Instead of providing resources and manufactured goods, Canada will increasingly supply technology, information, knowledge and expertise to the Third World, creating new career opportunities in the new sectors of the economy. Canada's future wealth is not beneath our feet, it's between our ears!

5. Building the Information Economy

The basic parts of the information sector *(see Figure 5)* have a great influence throughout the economy, creating jobs everywhere *(see Figure 6)*.

The 4th-Wave sector has strong export potential in a broad range of information activities. Very often, however, these potentials are overlooked. For example, in the 1st-Wave farming, forestry, fishing, mining and energy sectors, there is a wealth of technology and experience. Expertise on animal/plant breeding, land cultivation, geological exploration and mineral refining is embedded in these sectors. It needs to be dug out, packaged and transferred to a world desperate for knowledge and expertise.

The 2nd-Wave manufacturing sector is also becoming a key information supplier. Companies such as Bata already use electronic systems to pass product design information between units in different countries; these companies are becoming manufacturing databases, which are also linked to subcontractors and customers. As markets globalize, so do these electronic information links. In terms of information and knowledge content and work actually performed, futuristic manufacturers are becoming information-service conglomerates.

In this new economy, the more information one produces, the more one can produce because knowledge begets more knowledge. Because all real wealth stems from information (used to achieve efficiency) we can now generate exponential growth in wealth. We can increase economic (that is knowledge) production without limit and without damage to the environment.

Fig.5 Components of the Information Economy	
Information Business	**Non-Info Business**
Commercial Info: (production and sale)	*Info in Industry:* (produced within firms) Robotics, CAD/CAM, personal computers, word processors, calculators, copy machines, point-of-sale terminals, banking machines, etc.
Business Consumption: • Postal/courier service; business books/newspapers; • Magazines on technology and economy; • Printing, telephone, fax, and on-line services; • Database, computer network, software services.	*Info in Government:* (production, presentation, consumption) • Telecom systems; • Purchases from industry; • Info dissemination; • Education system; • Libraries.
Personal Consumption: • Postal service; • Newspaper/book/magazine; • Telephone/fax, radio/TV, computer services.	*Info in the Home:* • Consumption of all kinds of commercial, entertainment, and government information services.

(Source: *Jetro Newsletter*, Tokyo, 1990.)

Fig.6
Career-Related Information Industries

Information Industries	Privately-run info firms	Investigators, freelance writers, credit checkers, public opinion surveyors.
	Printers and publishers	Printing, plate making, bookbinding, publishing, photocopying, editing.
	News and advertising	Newspapers, news agencies, magazines, advertising, public relations.
	Info processing services	Computer centres, data banks, software houses, time sharing services.
	Info equipment makers	Printing presses, personal computers, terminal equipment, photocopiers.
Knowledge Industries	Knowledge firms	Lawyers, accountants, consultants, assessors, designers.
	Research firms	Think-tanks, research institutes, laboratories, engineering firms.
	Education sector	Schools/colleges/universities, seminars/training courses, libraries.
	Equipment suppliers	Research equipment, computers, calculators, teaching materials/equipment.
Arts Industries	Creative individuals	Novelists, composers, singers, painters, photographers, producers.
	Service companies	Theatre troupes, orchestras, movie studios, TV companies, theatres.
	Equipment suppliers	Photograph/TV equipment, musical instruments, film/recording equipment.
Ethics Industries	Ethicists	Philosophers, religious leaders.
	Shrines	Churches, temples, synagogues, etc.
	Spiritual retreats	Spiritual training centres/retreats, calligraphy/yoga/zen training, etc.

(Source: Adapted from Yoneji Masuda, *The Information Society*; reprinted with permission)

Because information is a plentiful factor of production, this decreases the cost of goods. As a result, the traditional 1st-Wave natural resource and 2nd-Wave manufacturing sectors of the economy are declining, while the 4th-Wave information economy booms.

Information is virtually the mirror-image of all previous commodities. Information also is power. The old adage "knowledge is power" has at last become literally true. Now, "what one knows" and/or "knowing where to find knowledge" (rather than "what one owns") is the key to future life success.

The Canadian education and information industries will be the twin pillars of Canada's information society. The new emphasis is on the consumption of information and knowledge, rather than the consumption of commodities. Indeed, in a real-time (instantaneous) environment, it is information (not time) that is money and money can be created nonstop, 24-hrs/day, 365-days/year.

That's the magic of information—and the key to our future prosperity, both individually and as a nation.

Political ("High-Virtue") Dynamics of Change

Social, technical and economic forces drive all societies towards essential political reform. In Canada, we are presently trapped in outmoded concepts of governance, which are stifled in bureaucracy—a natural outgrowth of the 2nd-Wave manufacturing society where the factory model became pervasive, resulting in mass education, central banking and national governments with mechanistic bureaucracies.

Today's political system is uncoupled from the new information economy. In the 1980s, Canadian politics degenerated into a quagmire of corrupt and unethical behaviour. The greed driven decade led to a total neglect of public concern: issues of the environment and the budget deficit were ignored while politicians slopped at the trough. The 1990s are the clean-up decade: a sweeping housecleaning and attention to areas of previous neglect as we prepare the country for the 21st century. Our political infrastructure will change dramatically in the late-1990s, driven by the following dynamics.

1. Shift from Party Politics to Issue Politics

With the knowledge explosion, voters are as informed as their representatives The 4th-Wave information society demands that political leaders show that they know what on earth is going on and are taking effective action.

The more educated people become, the more they want to do more than just elect decision-makers. People want another lever (other than voting) over their political leaders. This is reflected in political activism. With the rise of special interest groups and federations of different issues movements, political parties are less effective in meeting this need. Voters are looking for leaders that care more about solving problems than debating party ideology.

Party politics is being replaced by issue politics. It is the party of the day that most effectively tackles the issues of the day, that gains most public support.

2. Electronic Voting

The telecom revolution also is changing political processes and forcing us to devise new political theories. Democracy is not dead, but some of our ways of practicing it are obsolete. Computers are fast creating a world where citizens of the future will be able to participate not merely once but repeatedly. Since 1979, the number of computers in North American homes has grown from zero to more than 35-million. The late-1990s will see an explosion in home computer use; by the year 2005, 10-million PCs could be in home operation in Canada alone—each of them more advanced, easier to use and more powerful.

PCs "empower" people to create, manipulate, store, receive and transmit information and knowledge, thereby providing independence from traditional media. Personal computers also will give people power over governments—to monitor their activities and use databases that affect government decisions. By the year 2000, we will vote electronically in elections, from home. The electronic voting system will create thousands of jobs for computer technicians and political issues analysts and advisors.

3. Defusing the Ecology Bomb
We have been destroying the natural environment and creating ecological deficits. Belatedly, in the late-1980s, governments from the global to the local level began to recognize this problem. Consumer and industrial waste treatment and recycling programs will continue to be the rage. The "Mini-Depression," of course, slowed environmental efforts but thousands of new jobs will be created in restoring the environment and in monitoring the clean-up in the late-1990s.

4. Human Rights Issues
The struggle for human rights around such workplace issues as equal pay for work of equal value and sexual harassment continued in the 1980s. The 1990s saw these issues come to full fruition with rights being legislated across the board as the Charter of Rights and Freedoms became more-clearly defined through legal decisions. True workplace equity will evolve by the year 2000, but not before it has created lots of work for lawyers and human resource professionals, among others.

5. Government Decentralization
National legislative affairs are being refocussed. Matters of global concern will fully occupy the federal government in future. All other matters will increasingly be decentralized to the provincial and/or municipal levels of government, that is, to the level closest to where those matters need to be addressed. This will shift government employment in parallel. It will also create new, additional jobs at the lower levels of government.

6. Workplace Reform

In response to new social values, new technologies, and the roller-coaster economy, legislation relative to the workplace will be changed. The unemployment insurance program (UIC) will continue to be reformed in favour of training and hiring incentives, along lines I suggested earlier. Training credits and workplace leave entitlements will become the norm, just like sick leave. Regulations around the use of technology and guidelines about working at home will be instituted. Finally, but not least, statutory working hours will be reduced to 30-hours a week by the year 2000.

Let's face it, taken together these 4-STEP dynamics of change are creating a new Canada.

An old Chinese curse says *"May you live in interesting times."* Indeed, we are living in interesting times. But these also are exciting times. And, against this background of change, we can now identify the best career opportunities of the late-1990s and beyond.

Section B

Industry-by-Industry
Career Prospect Review

Based on what's *really* going on in the world, you should ignore most everything the Canadian government tells you in *JOB FUTURES* about where the best jobs will be. Here are the facts about the best future career prospects. You'll find your new career is in this section.

Drawing on the background of the changing workplace, this section provides an overview—and detailed listings—of career "families" and individual job titles in the six waves of the Canadian economy as follows:

- 1st-Wave: Agriculture/Natural Resources/Energy
- 2nd-Wave: Industry/Manufacturing/Robotics
- 3rd-Wave: Financial/Healthcare/Personal Services
- 4th-Wave: Information/Knowledge/High-Tech
- 5th-Wave: Leisure/Tourism
- 6th-Wave: Outer-Space

Scattered throughout each segment are job/career lists which highlight the realistically "bright side" of each occupational group. If a traditional job title is not listed, it is safe to assume that its outlook is dismal or, at best, below average.

By integrating all available future trends information, I also have developed specific growth forecasts to the year 2005 for all major job titles. That list is provided later, in Section C.

1st-Wave Careers:

Best Prospects in
Agriculture/Natural Resources/Energy

The 1st-Wave of the Canadian economy is less and less competitive in the global marketplace. Whether you look at farming, fishing, forestry, mining, or energy, all are faced with overcapacity in terms of domestic demand and their products are too expensive in world markets.

High-tech developments—such as bio-technology, genetics, computerization, informatics, and electronics—will continue to revolutionize this sector. The companies that survive and prosper will be those that go as "high-tech" as possible, position themselves in unique niches in the rapidly-changing global marketplace, and focus especially on selling their expertise and knowledge abroad.

There thus will be no overall long-term incremental domestic job growth in most of these sectors, especially near the production end of activity. Nearer the consumer end, in agrifood for example, we shall continue to see new product niches being opened up—and new careers in marketing, food nutrition, home economics and fast-food service. However, these jobs are in the more advanced waves of the economy and will be discussed later.

Let's examine the prospects for each sector of the 1st-Wave economy in turn.

Farming
Farming in the future depends on developing yet more efficient ways of growing even greater amounts of food on larger and larger farms—with fewer and fewer people being involved in the process. Traditional farmers, apart from horticulturists and

a relatively few growers of organic or other specialty crops, will virtually disappear from the Canadian agricultural landscape in the late-1990s. Most farmers and farm workers who retire or leave traditional farming simply will not be replaced.

Modern farmers must be expert soil and animal scientists, agronomists, engineers, business managers and marketers. They will design new farms and "invent" new crops which yield more nutritious food. Farming is going through yet another technological revolution. First, horses replaced human labour and then tractors replaced horses. Then farms adopted factory-like methods to raise animals in confined centralized areas. Now, farmers use computers (to plan crops and track yields) and robots (to drive planters, combines and fruit pickers, and to feed animals). In the late-1990s, robots will replace most of today's tractors and machines. The genetic revolution will let bio-engineers clone plants and vegetables that grow by the million in half the time it takes today. They'll also breed yet more hybrid animals to yield yet more nutritious food.

Clearly, the futuristic farm is very high-tech, and it's also clear where the best jobs will be. The best new farming careers for the late-1990s are:

- Animal Biologists/Breeders - Computer Programmers
- Geneticists   - Marketing Professionals
- Plant Biologists/Breeders - Roboticists

Fishing
Even if depleted fish stocks can be restored, Canadian fishing will remain highly vulnerable to technical change. The spread of huge factory-like freezer trawlers (floating fish factories) are replacing small fishing boats. This eliminates the jobs of most captains, boatswains, mates, pilots, navigators, marine engineers and skippers of fishing vessels. There is a corresponding decline in the need for boat carpenters, marine machinists, ship joiners, steel fitters and shipwrights. The manual labour of fish processing plant personnel also will be eliminated by yet more

sophisticated and fully-automated processing lines, both on land and on the floating fish plants.

The futuristic way of fishing is aquaculture or intensive fish farming. In parallel with the trend toward increased consumption of fish and other seafood in the strongly health-conscious North American and other markets, there will be a large number of new jobs created in this area throughout the late-1990s. The best jobs will go to:

- Fish Breeders
- Marketing Professionals
- Geneticists
- Marine Biologists

Ocean Industry

Aquaculture is also part of the new "sub-sea" or ocean industry. Other fields include marine transportation and related services, seabed mining, and marine science—and technology development in those areas. As with aquaculture, the primary job-creation obviously will occur in British Columbia and the Atlantic provinces. In the next decade, there will be a demand for some 5,000 people as:

- Camera Operators
- Chemists
- Computer Programmers
- Draftspersons
- Geophysicists
- Metallurgists
- Oceanographers
- Seismologists
- Chemical Engineers
- Civil Engineers
- Divers
- Electrical Engineers
- Marine Engineers
- Meteorologists
- Physicists
- Sonar Operators

Forestry

Forestry in Canada is a mature industry and increasingly automated. Therefore the demand for log graders, tree scalers and heavy equipment operators will continue to be very weak. As well, most of the saw mills and pulp and paper mills are becoming highly automated, with laser-guided saws and robotic log-handlers replacing most human labour in the production of wood and paper products. However, this sector is still a major

contributor to the overall economy and, with timber resources diminishing (and concerns about the environment increasing) in the late-1990s there will be a demand for forestry and timber professionals such as:
- Conservationists
- Silviculturists
- Genetic Engineers
- Wildlife Biologists

Mining
Canada's mining industry also will continue to decline in the Information Age. The metal-bashing era is over. Users of raw materials are switching to cheaper and often superior substitutes, from plastic to ceramic. The sector also is uncompetitive in the global marketplace. The struggle for efficiency means that bio-technological leaching, high-tech equipment, and robots are replacing people. Drillers and blasters of all kinds, along with most mining and petroleum engineers, will virtually disappear by the year 2000.

Still, the mining sector will require roboticists and computer mining professionals of various types. But the best job action in the late-1990s will be in the new area of "materials science" where there is a demand for:
- Jet Turbine Engineers
- Mineralogists
- Plastics Engineers
- Metallurgists
- New Material Developers
- Polymerization Scientists

Energy
The energy sector will boom again—but not in the same way as before. Due to the oil and energy glut of the late-1980s, the energy sector reduced employment as it downscaled its activities. And, while oil resources in North America are diminishing and becoming increasingly expensive to extract, the entire world is gradually "going off" oil and coal, switching instead to other non-polluting fuels, particularly natural gas. Canada has huge reserves of natural gas which it will increasingly sell to the U.S. market along with hydro- and nuclear-generated electricity.

Despite the bad press received by nuclear power, the system is expanding and scientists are finding ways to safely store nuclear fuel and decommission obsolete plants. Long-term energy demand creates the prospect of a boom in alternate sources of energy. In the late-1990s, careers in alternate fuel sources will boom: solar, geothermal, synfuels, wind, biomass, and (sometime after the year 2000) super-conductivity and nuclear fusion. The jobs in greatest demand in the Canadian energy sector in the late-1990s are:

- Accelerator Operators
- Radiochemists
- Electronics Engineers
- Energy Conservationits
- Hazardous Waste Engineer
- Isotope Plant Operators
- Nuclear Radiologists
- Power Line Installers
- Radiochem. Lab. Aides

- Chemical Engineers
- Computer Professionals
- Energy Auditors
- Gamma Plant Operators
- Hydrologists
- New Material Engineers
- Nuclear Physicists
- Power Plant Operators
- Solar Cell Technicians

By the way, house and factory electric meter readers are being replaced by automated systems. By the year 2000, most meters will be read electronically from a central location by computer via in-home cable/telephone lines.

Environmental Protection
Environment-related careers have become more and more appealing as people continue to press for protection of natural resources. People who study, manage and conserve the resources of earth, air and water—and solve garbage problems—will be in great demand throughout the 21st century.

Many of these jobs are in government. National, provincial and local govrnments have a prime responsibility in setting and monitoring environmental standards. Other jobs are appearing in all sectors of industry, from 1st-Wave to 6th-Wave, as companies adopt "green" manufacturing processes and products. A variety of trained specialists also are needed to solve acid rain and other environmental problems. These trends create openings for:

- Air Quality Specialists   - Botanists
- Chemists   - Ecologists
- Environmental Accountants   - Environmental Consultants
- Environmental Engineers   - Forest Agrologists
- Forensic Accountants   - Hydrologists
- Meteorologists   - Naturalists
- Recycling Coordinators   - Toxicologists
- Zoologists

2nd-Wave Careers:

Best Prospects in
Industry/Manufacturing/Robotics

As explained earlier, the heavy industrial and manufacturing activity of the world is shifting rapidly to Mexico and the Third World. As a result, the Canadian manufacturing sector continues to reduce overall plant capacity.

This does not mean that Canadian manufacturing is entirely defunct. But the old jobs simply will not come back again. There will be lower than average demand for factory/plant managers and metallurgical and mechanical/stationary engineers of all kinds. The need for machinists, tool-and-die makers, sheet metal workers, welders, boiler makers, inspectors and testers will decline dramatically. So will that for "back room" office jobs such as production clerks, shipping/receiving clerks, and inventory clerks. On the production line itself, assemblers and packers are being eliminated by automation.

Rather than lathes, blast furnaces and extrusion machines, the tools of new manufacturing will be lasers, microwaves, fiber optics, nuclear power, parallel processing, particle accelerators, artificial intelligence and super-conductors. Robots and computers will continue to replace humans wherever possible. Overall, Canadian manufacturing will lose more than 100,000 jobs over the next 12 years. Those jobs that remain will increasingly be knowledge jobs in a high-tech world.

Robotics
There is a bright career future in robotics. Until 1960, robots were science fiction. By 1993, there were more than 8,000 in place in Canada and 600,000 worldwide. Robots work on assembly lines (even in water or underground) replacing human labour. They do hazardous tasks such as spraying paint or handling chemicals or nuclear fuel which are unsafe for humans to handle. Old-fashioned lathe operators, welders, assemblers and painters are simply disappearing.

But robots also create thousands of new jobs. There are more than 3,000 firms in the North American robotics and computer aided design and manufacturing (CAD/CAM) industries. They employ 1.1-million people who research, plan, design, manufacture, sell, deliver, install, generate and maintain industrial robots. By the year 2005, there will be more than 12,000 industrial robots in Canada and another 10,000 home robots could also be bought by consumers.

Robots are already commonplace in the automobile industry and will become more so in the aerospace, electronics, pharmaceutical, food processing, health and physical therapy fields. Over half of the robotics jobs are either engineering or technically oriented:

- CAD/CAM Engineers
- CIM Engineers
- Electronics Engineers
- Holographic Inspectors
- Laser Technicians
- Mechanical Engineers
- Optical Engineers

- Chemical Engineers
- Computer Repairers
- Engineering Technicians
- Instrument Technicians
- Materials Specialists
- New Materials Engineers
- Research/Engineering Aides

- Robotics Engineers   - Robotics Repairers
- Robot Supervisors

Textiles

As with the other 2nd-Wave sectors, the textile industry also is losing market share to foreign suppliers, and still more thousands of Canadian workers will lose their jobs in this sector. Most exposed are designers, pattern-makers, cutters and punchers. Garment printing will also start to be done by xerography (like a photocopy machine) by the late-1990s, replacing T-shirt printers and table cloth, drape and fashion silk screeners. Even custom tailors and dressmakers, while filling a profitable niche, are in over-supply and will face fierce competition to survive. Most in demand are:
- CAD Designers   - Private Label Personnel
- Small Boutique Personnel

Chemicals

The petro-chemical industry faces stiff competition from new Saudi Arabian refineries coming on stream. As a result the demand for refinery managers and chemists of all kinds in Canada is flat. The exceptions are organic and polymer chemists, but these are really 4th-Wave high-tech careers.

Transportation

In the 2nd-Wave manufacturing age, we mainly moved goods around. While we still need to do that, in the 4th-Wave information age we mainly will move information around. As manufacturing wanes, related transportation employment must decline. Railroad employment, for example, continues to be halved every 25-years, and the slashing of VIA Rail services across Canada has exacerbated this trend. Ships now have skeleton crews and a computer that looks after the vessel. Many courier company drivers will be put out of business by FAX machines and computer modems. Parcel delivery and long-distance goods drivers will still be in demand. However,

this sector is not growing: larger trucks reduce the number of
drivers required and automated material handling eases freight
movement.

The exception to these trends is the people-moving business:
urban transit of all kinds. Even though the workplace is being
decentralized away from downtown and many people are working from home, there will be a continued surge in the demand
for urban and suburban transit. As well, the 5th-Wave leisure
and tourism boom will continue to create an ongoing job dem-
and. The best transport sector jobs in the late-1990s are:
- Airline Crew Members   - Airline Managers
- Airline Pilots   - Airplane Navigators
- Airport Managers   - Airport Personnel
- Air Traffic Controllers - Bus/Transit Operators
- Rental Car Personnel   - Taxi Drivers

Construction
There still is a need for civil engineers and surveyors, but the
mega-project days of oil refineries and industrial complexes are
over in Canada. Existing industrial buildings need to be main-
tained but little new construction will occur. Similarly, there
is a glut of office buildings and shopping centres. However,
the construction sector requires people to meet residential,
information sector, healthcare, and leisure sector demands.

The ongoing boom in the these sectors, however, will not
be as labour-intensive as in the past. Much of the actual material preparation is being moved to pre-assembly or pre-fab processes in automated factories.

In future, even on construction sites, many humans will be
replaced by robots. Concrete mixers already can pump concrete as high as 25-storeys, eliminating the handling problem
on the ground. In Japan, robots are used to erect steel beams
and insert and tighten the connecting bolts. Other robots raise
and plaster walls, lay bricks, smooth concrete floors and install
windows. Future construction job openings are brightest for
fine craftspeople and finishers and those working on building

rehabilitation and restoration. As well, there is a high demand for:

- Air Conditioning Experts   - Architects
- Carpenters   - Electrical Engineers
- Fibre Optics Installers   - Landscapers
- Project/Leasing Managers   - Real Estate Agents

Most of the best jobs will be in the suburban centres, and municipal/urban planners will also be in high demand, as discussed in the next segment.

3rd-Wave Careers:

Best Prospects in
Financial/Healthcare/Personal Services

Everything we do, from morning till night, is made possible by people working in the service economy: in a bank, doctor's office, dry cleaning or other service outlet.

The 3rd-Wave service sector grew to become the largest employer in the Canadian economy in 1950 and remained so until about 1980. While many service jobs are now being replaced by 4th-Wave information/high-tech and 5th-Wave leisure jobs, there is still a strong future in the service sector of the economy.

This sector will continue to provide career opportunities galore, from the unskilled to the most highly-skilled professional. However, because of the employment restructuring taking place, career choices in the late-1990s must be made knowledgeably and with foresight.

Healthcare Industry
There is no better time to enter the health profession. More than any other part of Canada's 6-wave economy, the healthcare field offers the most outstanding job growth and many of the best jobs. Today, as many as one in nine new jobs in the U.S.A. and Canada are health-related. More than 400,000 additional workers should join the healthcare industry between 1994 and 2005. By then, there also will be five or six nonmedical professionals in support of every seven physicians. Jobs in residential care should grow faster than any other industry sector, at 7.2% a year.

The major reason for this amazing career outlook is that Canada has an increasingly health-conscious and (more important) aging population. This creates a huge demand for healthcare workers of all kinds, offering a wide range of career openings, from those with low skill levels to the most educated medical practitioners.

Many other fast-growing job types are indirectly related to healthcare. Eldercare is gradually replacing childcare as the primary focus of Baby Boomers because they have more aging relatives than children, and their children will soon be grown up anyway. Nursing homes already outnumber hospitals by more than two to one. They will hire more healthcare professionals, nurses, technical assistants and therapists.

Healthcare career openings clearly vary in parallel with society's changing health needs, changing technology, disease prominence, and changes in specialization. For example, since Baby Boomers delayed parenthood and limited the number of their children, this narrowed the need for obstetricians and pediatricians.

Conversely, until cancer is cured (which could occur in the late-1990s) there will be an ongoing demand for oncologists. A fast-growing surgical sub-specialty is same-day surgery to conduct hernia, cataract and foot operations. "Bloodless surgery" using advanced lasers will reduce patient trauma and cut hospital stays.

As well, there is a demand for healthcare workers who can tend people at home. Home care will see faster growth than any other profession between now and 2005. Thus, while the health field will offer prestigious and lucrative careers, you must be wary of these shifts in emphasis as society changes.

The healthcare profession, of course, is controlled by doctors. Much of this control is based on their custody of advanced medical knowledge. In turn, this guarantees their high incomes. To preserve their control, doctors claim that there will be a *surplus* of doctors in Canada in the late-1990s. This is sheer nonsense! Due to the aging population, there will be a severe *shortage* of doctors in Canada and no young Canadian should be dissuaded from entering the medical field as a physician or other specialist. Even then, the demand for healthcare will increase, not diminish, healthcare incomes.

However, the doctors' preserve over much of their knowledge will gradually erode. Everyday medical knowledge is becoming, well, everyday. With advances in medical technology, an increasingly educated society can simply do much of its own doctoring, often using medical kits at home, and so avoiding the need to visit the doctor on routine matters. Where this is not the case, nurses and other paramedics will be allowed to take on general medical tasks. Therefore, general medicine is changing, with much work being spun off to medics other than doctors, especially nurses or nurse practitioners.

The demand for Canadian nurses also is increasing due to changing patterns of nursing-school enrollment in the United States. Enrollment there fell 40% between 1983 and 1993 and could decline another 10% by 2000. Every graduate of a U.S. nurse practitioner training program has 6 to 8 jobs waiting.

This draws Canadian nurses to the U.S. and creates thousands of nursing openings, at higher salaries, across Canada. Many nurses in the U.S. now work for employment agencies and travel for several weeks or months to fill-in at hospitals unable to recruit full-time staff. The same trend is coming to Canada.

Hence, the Canadian nursing profession will continue to grow at 6%/year just to keep up with demand. And, while 65% of today's nurses work in a hospital setting, by the year 2005 only 35% might do so. As hinted above, the majority will work in nursing homes, corporate medical offices, health maintenance organizations (HMOs), and community medical centres. As cost containment and diagnostic related groups (DRGs) encourage hospitals to discharge patients sooner in order to cut costs, more nurses will be required to provide home recuperation and ambulatory care. Others will become marketing reps for pharmaceutical firms or nurse-lawyers in major law firms.

An important aspect of healthcare, of course, is dental care. Dentistry will remain a well-paying career into the next century but, again, there are some shifts to be aware of. Certain decay prevention measures could negate the need for regular dental care altogether. People have fewer cavities due to fluoridation of water and better dental care.

But an aging society faces periodontic (gum) disease and worn-down teeth that need restoration or replacement with caps and implants. This is creating a new profession of geriatric dentistry. Still, as people age, they want to preserve their teeth. This is creating a large demand for dental hygienists. Advances in cosmetic and periodontal dentistry also have created a need for various specialists as well as general dentists.

Against this background, it's easy to see that virtually any type of healthcare job will be at the top of any list of "best jobs" because, quite simply, there is huge demand everywhere for healthcare professionals. For example, more than 75% of companies now offer stop-smoking, stress control, and other prevention programs. Dieticians also conduct corporate nutrition seminars, advise food companies on marketing strategies, and teach healthy-eating classes. Also note that healthcare is a recession-proof industry because most people always pay attention to their health.

Here, then, is a list of the best Canadian jobs in healthcare for the late-1990s—and beyond:

- Hospital Administrators
- Health Service Managers
- Acupuncturists
- Cryobiologists
- Geriatricians
- Gynecologists
- Obstetricians
- Physicians
- Surgical Nurses

- Nursing Home Managers
- Medical Record Managers
- Anesthesiologists
- Gastroenterologists
- Gerontologists
- Laser Surgeons
- Pediatricians
- Surgeons
- Travelling Surgical Nurses

- Chiropractors/Osteopaths
- Osteopathic Physicians
- Sports Physicians

- Orthopaedic Surgeons
- Podiatrists

- Ambulatory Personnel
- Geriatric Nurses
- Integrated Care Deliverers
- Nurse Anesthetists
- Nursing Aides/Orderlies
- Outpatient Personnel
- Registered Nurses
- Travelling Nurses

- Corporate Nurses
- Home Health Nurses
- Licensed Practical Nurses
- Nurse Lawyers
- Nurse Practitioners
- Paramedic Personnel
- School Nurses

- Occupational Therapists
- Physical Therapists
- Prostheticians
- Rehabilitation Therapists
- Speech Pathologists

- Occupational Therapy Assts.
- Physical Therapist Assistants
- Recreational Therapists
- Respiratory Therapists
- Therapeutic Recreationalists

- Diagnostic Programmers
- ECG Technicians
- Emergency Medical Aides
- Laser Therapists
- Medical Laboratory Aides
- Oncologists
- PET/CAT Scan Aides

- Dialysis Technicians
- EEG Technicians
- Hematologists
- MDI Technicians
- Medical Records Clerks
- Operating Room Technicians
- X-ray Technologists

- Dietitians   - Nutritionists

- Pharmacists (see also 4th-Wave)

- Alcohol/Drug Abuse Aides - Child Psychologists
- Geriatric Psychologists   - Neuropsychologists
- Psychologists   - Psychiatrists
- Rehabilitation Psychologists - Social Workers
- Wellness Consultants

- Childcare Aides   - Domestic Aides
- Eldercare Aides   - Maids
- Medical Centre Cleaners   - Medical Centre Custodians

- Dentists   - Dental Assistants
- Dental Hygienists   - Dental Lab Technicians
- Endodontists   - Geriatric Dentists
- Oral Pathologists   - Oral Radiologists
- Oral Surgeons   - Paedodontists
- Prosthodontists   - Orthodontists

- Dispensing Opticians   - Ophthalmologists
- Ophthalmic Therapists   - Optometrists
- Optometric Assistants

Social & Community Service

Closely related to healthcare is social work, which cuts across many job boundaries. Social welfare, criminal justice, mental health, home economics and community service are the main areas of future growth. Again, information technology is transforming many public service jobs.

For example, paperwork—the bane of police officers—is being replaced by databases where cops hunt for clues. Automated traffic management systems are smoothing traffic flows and identifying offenders. The patrol car is a mobile crime lab linked to a central crime technology centre.

Overall, the best social work career paths in the late-1990s in Canada are:

- Adoption Agents   - Alcohol/Drug Abuse Aides
- Anthropologists   - Ethnologists
- Family Counsellors   - Hot Line Counsellors
- Retirement Counsellors   - Sex Therapists
- Social Psychiatrists   - Social Psychologists
- Social Researchers   - Sociobiologists
- Sociologists   - Urban Sociologists
- Welfare Agency Managers

- Dieticians   - Domestic Aides
- Fashion Designers   - Financial Counsellors
- Fitness Consultants   - Geriatric Workers
- Home Economists   - Interior Designers
- Nutritionists   - Voluntary Agency Managers

- Ambulance Drivers   - Emergency Service Personnel
- Fire Fighters   - Paramedics

- Police Officers   - Computer Crime Detectives
- Database Managers   - Criminologists
- Customs Officers   - Drug Busters
- Immigration Officers   - Parole Officers
- Public Security Guards   - Refugee Counsellors

Community Planning
With the spread of suburban living comes the need to improve community planning, design, and management. The various professions involved in community planning offer some of the best career paths. Examples include:
- Architects/Surveyors   - Building/Facilities Managers

- Town Centre Managers   - Community Info Personnel
- Community Planners   - Traffic Control Engineers
- Environment Assessors   - Landscape Architects
- Land Use Surveyors   - Leasing Agents
- Park Designers   - Real Estate Professionals
- Leisure Centre Mgrs.   - Transportation Planners
- Urban Designers

Human Resource Professions

Keeping employees happy and productive is becoming a more and more important priority. Jobs in the human resources sector could increase 30% or more during the next decade, and professionals in this field will become more important in the business world. Affirmative action (equal rights and pay, regardless of age, sex or race), technological change, and the end of the huge wave of Baby Boom job entrants, are forcing employers to focus increasing attention on human resource development as a primary organizational function. The vast need for training and retraining also is creating demand for professionals in this field.

Of course, faced with a shrinking labour supply—and company downsizing to restore efficiency—many employers are turning to "employee leasing" firms and placement agencies. Some employers are completely turning their entire human resource management function over to sub-contracted agencies. Therefore, while the demand for human resource development and training (HRDT) professionals will grow strongly, some of that growth will occur in these agencies, not in the public or private sector employers themselves. The best HRDT career openings in Canada in the late-1990s are as follows:

- Employee Lease Mgrs.   - Employee Relations Officers
- Outplacement Advisors - Placement Agency Professionals
- Recruitment Officers   - Relocation Counsellors
- Retirement Counsellors - Salary/Benefit Administrators
- Telecommuter Mgrs.   - Training/Development Officers

Secretarial and Office Careers

As well, of course, the various employee leasing and part-time personnel agencies are looking for thousands of part-time and temporary employees. They are needed to fill positions at corporate and government clients in almost every other kind of organizational role that you can think of.

However, you should be aware that certain office jobs are likely to disappear in large numbers from Canadian offices during the late-1990s:

● "Paper shufflers" (such as credit card clerks) will be replaced by sophisticated computer systems which handle transactions electronically from point-of-sale terminals, eliminating the need for credit card chits.

● Bookkeepers (as distinct from accountants or auditors) are being automated out of existence.

In contrast, the number of secretarial positions continues to grow dramatically. While one computer/word-processor replaced 2 typewriters, such technologies enable service and information suppliers to do things that previously were not possible, thus leading to an ongoing demand for secretarial workers. Their number will continue to grow as new businesses start up and as existing ones expand.

Looking further ahead, however, just as word-processors replacing typewriters in the 1980s, secretaries who use word-processors may be replaced by yet more sophisticated computers and voice-activated technologies such as "speak-writers" in the late-1990s.

Sophisticated telephone answering devices are also starting to replace telephone receptionists and appointment clerks *(discussed later)*. On balance, the best office careers for the late-1990s are:

- Admin. Assistants   - Admin. Secretaries
- Wordprocessors   - Receptionists (Personal)

Other Services
Other noteworthy service sector employment opportunities are:

● Public Services
In every Canadian community, in addition to the public services already discussed, there will be an ever-increasing need for public utility services: hydro, gas, water, sewers, garbage disposal and recycling, street upkeep and cleaning, parks and sports complex maintenance, and (especially) environmental clean-up and restoration. While automation is replacing some mundane and boring jobs in these fields (for example, hydro meter reading, mentioned earlier), these civic areas present expanding career options for low-skilled workers.

● Janitorial Services
There is a huge demand for janitors, cleaners, housekeepers, groundskeepers, and similar jobs in every sector of the economy.

● Mechanic and Repair Services
Unfortunately, the demand for mechanics and repairpersons is constantly declining. Everything—airplanes, cars, robots, household appliances, personal computers, telephones, watches—is increasingly reliable and requires less and less repair and service. Many of these jobs (for example, watch repairing) are simply going the way of the blacksmith.

Low-Tech Job Opportunities
In an increasingly high-tech world, many people are fearful of the career market because they feel they lack the necessary aptitude or technical background. As indicated above, however, there are thousands of jobs that do *not* require a degree in science, engineering, mathematics or computers. All of them

are vitally important jobs that employers in all 6-waves of the Canadian economy need done in a competent manner.

Every employer needs "behind-the-scenes" and "low-tech" people; people who do jobs indirectly related to scientific endeavour, but still of vital importance. These jobs, often called "staff" or "back office" positions, should be pursued by those with the appropriate skills:

- Payroll Accountants
- Sales/Mktg. Personnel
- Technical Writers
- Assembly Workers
- Stock Clerks

- Secretaries/Wordprocessors
- Public Affairs Specialists
- Production Technicians
- Purchasing Officers

Note that while some of these jobs are disappearing from many sectors of the Canadian economy, many often are found in small and middle-sized companies that do not use (and do not plan to use) highly-automated administrative systems. In addition, of course, even the 4th-Wave high-tech companies require many people in these fields. Such firms, as I shall discuss next, are also likely to be so wealthy that they will be able to pay higher salaries for these jobs than would a company in a declining industry. But, as I also shall outline in a later section, these jobs will increasingly require at least a High School Diploma, and probably some further education too. Moreover, all jobs—whether high-tech or low-tech—require the ability to at least use a telephone and a computer terminal.

Electronic "Services-at-Home"

Cable and telecom networks already allow many of us to receive certain services at home from our armchair. Examples are banking at home and TV shopping.

By the year 2005, a large percentage of Canadians will receive the following "services-at-home" via their personal computer terminals and/or interactive TVs (ITVs):

% of Homes	Service Accessed
85	Addresses/Telephone Numbers
80	Catalogue/ITV/PC Shopping
80	Directories of Goods/Services
80	Electronic Games
80	Personal Message Systems
80	Real Estate Listings
75	Library/Databank Services
75	Electronic Mail (E-mail)
70	Fast Food Orders
70	Home Security (Fire/Police/Burglar)
65	Restaurant Reservations
65	Travel/Hotel Reservations
60	Education/Retraining
60	Entertainment Bookings
60	Personalized News Reports
50	Banking/Financial Services
50	Community Info (By-Laws, etc)
50	Electronic Registration/Voting
50	Income Tax Filing
45	Routine Medical Diagnosis
40	Secretarial Services
30	Legal Advice
20	Translation Services

As such services become widespread in the late-1990s, thousands of jobs will be eliminated in libraries, ticket offices, etc.

At the same time, firms providing these services will require tens of thousands of tele-service professionals, computer programmers and back-up support personnel of various kinds. Working in "Call Centres," these people answer 800-number telephone calls to handle complaints, supply product information, take orders, and provide help in the use of products.

This electronic restructuring of the marketplace should be kept in mind in reviewing job options in the 3rd-Wave Service economy and in the information-oriented sectors of the 4th-Wave economy, discussed next.

4th-Wave Careers:

Best Prospects in
Information/Knowledge/High-Tech

Without question, information/knowledge and high-tech careers are the wave of the immediate future. As indicated earlier, we already are in the Information Age, and information/knowledge workers now comprise the largest sector of the Canadian workplace. The information revolution, of course, is not just propelled by the knowledge explosion but also by the high-tech revolution. Together, they are fueling the 4th-Wave boom as well as transforming the previous 1st-, 2nd-, and 3rd-Wave sectors of the economy.

What is high technology? All Canadians have experienced some form of technological change, perhaps at school, at work, or through products consumed. A microwave oven, for example, is in 70% of Canadian homes. A television and VCR with a remote control device is a piece of high-tech that all of us now take for granted. Personal computers (PCs) are finding their way onto desks in offices and schools, and into many homes. Thousands more do so every year.

Clearly, all these technologies require special knowledge by anyone having to function in the modern world. These stupendous technologies also open up unparalleled career openings. While many once-rewarding career fields are withering due to techno-change, the good news is that for every job field becoming obsolete, an exciting new field is popping up to take its place. Thousands of new Canadian jobs are in fields that simply didn't exist 10-years ago—and which, incidentally, are not even classified by the Canadian government.

Let's look first at the exciting prospects for information and knowledge workers—those who use tele-computer technologies to do their jobs. Information and knowledge workers are to be found in all sectors of the economy. Many of them are in specific fields of expertise such as the healthcare service sector I've already examined. Let's now look at some other brain-intensive fields.

Lawyers
The legal profession continues to be a sure-fire growth industry. As more and more people need legal services to sort out the complexities of modern life, lawyers as a group are in short supply. New experts are required to deal with new crimes such as information theft, copyright violations, and environmental damage. Mediators to solve sticky public issues also work through law firms and paralegal clinics.

There are thousands of jobs for paralegals in all branches of law. Paralegals, because they do not have law degrees, cannot give legal advice to clients or make legal decisions. But they are taking over many of the functions once handled by lawyers, such as notarizing papers or drafting and negotiating contracts. Many set up their own store-front legal offices to take away these bread-and-butter items from the traditional law firms.

As Canadian business goes global, spreading to the U.S., Mexico, Europe, Asia, and the Third World, specialists in international law are sought after. In particular there is a growing demand for people who understand the NAFTA agreement and the details of doing business in Europe and Russia. Others are required to understand the business of joint-ventures and technology transfers, especially with Mexico, Russia, Eastern Europe, China, the Philippines, Thailand, Vietnam and other reforming economies.

Reflecting the globalizing economy, the best legal careers in the late-1990s are in the following fields:
- Biotechnology Patents   - Computer Law
- Environmental Law   - Immigration
- Information   - Intellectual Property Rights
- International Taxation   - International Trade

Educators

Educators are the traditional creators of knowledge itself. In the Information Age, however, computer programs will do most of the teaching while educators facilitate learning.

The children of the Baby Boom generation (the "Shadow Boom" is working its way through our schools and so there is no decline in the need for educators. During the next decade, however, factory-style schools and colleges will become obsolete. With the onset of individualized (computerized) lifelong learning, at every level of education there will be a need for thousands upon thousands of learning facilitators, showing people where to find knowledge and how to apply it.

Educators also will be required to prepare people for the new high-growth career fields identified in this book. The demand for lifelong learning will mean that 5% of the workforce will be in retraining programs at any one time. Schools and colleges will educate children and retrain adults around the clock—often electronically via ITV and PC at home—providing 24-hour-a-day year-round access.

Interesting new areas of study will be: computational linguistics; information science management; Asian geography and culture; and languages such as Japanese, Chinese and Russian. But rarely will teachers instruct classes themselves. Instead they will be freed up to deliver personalized tutoring.

Career Counsellors

The restructuring of the career marketplace is dramatically increasing the demand for career counsellors. These specialists now work not just in education but in business, government and community agencies, and many operate their own consultancies. As everything in this book shows, they have an exceptionally bright future.

Librarians

Libraries are undergoing dramatic change and have become warehouses of information and knowledge. While books are technically obsolete, a "user-friendly" alternative is still not in sight. Nevertheless, the job of the librarian is and will continue to change. The extensive use of computers to store information and handle routine operations (cataloging and ordering) boosts the need for information and automation specialists.

Tomorrow's libraries are databases of knowledge to which users will refer by telecommuting from office, school or home via their PCs. In the late-1990s, the best library career prospects are for people specializing in scientific and technical fields, particularly in research libraries: computer abstractors, indexers, bibliography researchers, and archivists.

Publishers
Books have reached their zenith as a piece of info-storage technology. There were more than 65,000 new titles published in 1993 in Canada and the United States. This information explosion will continue as long as books remains the most "user-friendly" storage/retrieval technology for information and knowledge. Desk-top publishing programs for PCs also now make it possible for anyone to publish a book. Moreover, this technology makes it possible to custom-tailor books and periodicals to suit particular reader tastes. It also means that jobs such as proof-reading and typesetting are all done by computer. Also, more books will come with computer disks for those who prefer to copy the book onto their computer's hard drive.

The magazine industry will continue to fragment into specialized publications, with the next wave of changes involving a move to electronic custom-tailored publications for subscribers who will receive precisely what they want to read, via either PC modem or FAX. Consequently, the publishing industry is becoming very competitive and the survivors will be high-tech and very much involved in electronic publishing via telephone dial-up data bank services. The best career openings are in management, design, marketing and promotion, and database creation and management.

Information Brokers/Consultants

Management consulting is and will remain one of the fastest-growing professions. Society simply needs more and more guidance in coping with information overload, in managing information, in understanding how the world is changing, and in strategically managing that change. Information consultants provide expertise to the full range of organizational functions, especially strategic planners, marketers, human resource development officers, and public affairs executives.

Public relations has become the key interface between government, corporate and institutional entities and their publics. This has spawned a whole new profession called Issues Management, a profession that will grow in importance as various public issues need to be addressed. The best career options in this entire field include:

- Business Agents   - Business Communicators
- Consultants (all types) - Futurists
- Govt. Affairs Specialists - Information Officers/Clerks
- Issues Managers   - Promoters
- Publicists   - Public Affairs Executives
- Writers/Editors

Computer Professionals

In 1960, only 10,000 computers were in service worldwide. Today, 100-million computers are in use and their number is growing at 40% annually and should reach 12-million in Canada alone by the year 2000. Computers will be sitting on every desk and will be carried in briefcases, cars, pockets and purses by every Canadian. As common as telephones, they will store almost all of our knowledge. Already many computers obey spoken commands and, by the year 2000, it will be necessary only to know how to speak to a computer to retrieve, manipulate and transmit information in your day-to-day life.

During the late-1990s, jobs also will explode by 40%—especially in fields such as programming and systems analysis. Even this rate of growth may be conservative. There could be

100,000 new jobs for software writers alone in Canada by the year 2005. In the late-1990s, AI (artificial intelligence) experts, who create software to perform tasks involving almost-human thinking, will start to be in great demand. Computers already perform language translation activities. Some have performed brain surgery. As computers become more user-friendly, the number of computer and peripheral equipment operators should decline. The reason is a declining use of mainframe computers and a growing use of PCs.

By the year 2000, over 2-million Canadians will be working directly with computers. Another 800,000 will work directly in computer areas—more than double the 1988 figure. Some of the best careers in the computer field:

- AI Experts
- Chief Info. Officers
- Computational Linguists
- Computer Operators

- CAD/CAM Specialists
- Computer Security Officers
- Computer Engineers
- Computer Programmers
  (see caution below)

- Computer Sales Reps
- EDP Repairers
- Data Base Managers
- Graphic Designers
- Network Technicians
- Systems Engineers

- Computer System Analysts
- Data Processing Managers
- Engineering/Science Aides
- Information Managers
- Software Engineers
- Systems Integrators

A note of caution: Two trends could eliminate most computer programming jobs. First, advanced computers may be able to program themselves. Second, Third World countries such as China and India are becoming major suppliers of computer programming and software services—at a cost of only 10% of what these services cost in North America. Programming careers thus should be chosen with extreme caution.

On the other hand, specialized software and systems engineers are in demand. While software engineers need to know programming and software systems, they combine computer science, electrical engineering and business knowledge to work with accountants, cost managers and other business professionals to create large-scale corporate systems.

Similarly, systems engineers combine engineering, operations research, information systems management, statistics, cost control, accounting and advanced mathematics to play a major co-ordinating role in complex fields such as aerospace. These multi-facetted careers would therefore be much preferable to plain old computer programming careers which could be eliminated.

Telecommunications
Closely inter-related with computers is the telecom industry. Microelectronics, computers, fiber optics, lasers, and space satellites are expanding the reach of telecommunications. Entire industries are being spawned by these technologies. Through companies such as Northern Telecom, Canada has always been a leader in the field and, in today's global marketplace, the ability to effectively manage telecom technology is a strategic business resource. Canada also is experiencing an information explosion and various telecom media (computers, telephones, TV, PCs, FAX machines) are being integrated to exploit that information, manipulate it, and distribute it between people, homes and organizations. The major telephone and cable companies will provide most of the job openings in Canada in the late-1990s, as follows:

- Cable Installers
- Telecom Mgrs.
- Voting Machine Experts
- Fiber Optic Technicians
- Imaging Specialists
- Line Inspectors
- Sales/Mktg. Specialists
- Alarm System Installers
- Telecom Managers

- Communications Technicians
- Electronic Mail Technicians
- FAX Machine Repairers
- GIS Specialists
- Line Installers/Managers
- Network Managers
- Satellite Dish Technicians
- Switch Technicians
- Phone Equipment Repairers

- Transmitter Repairers   - Videotext Operators
- Wireless Specialists

Biotechnology
Also sometimes called bio-engineering, biotechnology (or bio-tech) involves genetic engineering, gene splicing and cloning to create new life forms and improve old ones. The field is nurturing a revolution that promises to transform dozens of other industries, from agriculture and mining to pharmaceuticals and pollution control. Biotech could even come to rival the development of computers. Biotech research work is already moving from the laboratory to the marketplace. In addition to new start-up companies, many old-line pharmaceutical, chemical and oil companies operate biotech subsidiaries. Biotech career opportunities fall into six main areas:

- Control of problems in raw-material-processing (such as pollution created by cellulose-processing);
- Modification of raw materials (such as making better wood pulp);
- Improvement of existing products (such as advanced pharmaceuticals);
- Production of new products (such as new proteins and bio-cosmetics);
- Management of waste residues (through such means as recycling); and
- Optimization of processing operations (such as inter-faces with computers and robotics).

As a young field, however, most of the jobs in biotech are still connected with the research end of things. But high-tech production will pave the way for still more jobs in the late-1990s and early years of the 21st century. Needed will be:

- Anatomists   - Applied Biologists
- Biochemists   - Biotechnicians
- Botanists   - Chemical Engineers
- Chemists   - Computer Programmers

- Ecologists	- Electrical Engineers
- Entomologists	- Geneticists
- Limnologists	- Mathematicians
- Medical Bacteriologists	- Medical Technologists
- Microbiologists	- Molecular Biologists
- Neurobiologists	- Organic Chemists
- Pathologists	- Pharmacologists
- Physiologists	- Protein Geometricians
- Recombnt DNA Experts	- Zoologists

Biomedical Technology

The bionic human is coming closer to reality as scientists, engineers, technicians, doctors and others team up to create medical miracles. They are developing artificial limbs and organs, diagnostic test equipment and surgical operating tools and equipment.

The field of biomedical technology (or biomed) is closely related to that of biotechnology. Many of the bionic implants and diagnostic tools are based on the biological compatibility and chemistry of the human body. Researchers are now working on artificial eyes, ears and mechanical kidneys.

There will be jobs galore in biomed in the late-1990s and early years of the next century, as follows:

- Assembly Technicians	- Biochemists
- Biomedical Engineers	- Ceramics Engineers
- Chemists	- Computer Personnel
- Engineers (all kinds)	- Laboratory Technicians
- Medical Technologists	- Radiology Medical Technicians
- Paramedics	- Pathologists
- Polymer Engineers	- Respiratory Therapists
- Surgical Technicians	

Pharmaceuticals

We are in the midst of an ongoing revolution in prescription drugs—formally called pharmaceuticals. About 80% of all the drugs ever invented have been developed since 1975. The next

20-years will see a major change in drug treatment as scientists unlock mysteries of the brain and find effective therapies for depression, schizophrenia and senility. Cures are also likely to be found for diabetes, arthritis, Alzheimer's disease, heart disease—and probably for cancer and AIDS.

As already discussed, healthcare is Canada's fastest-growing service industry. Spending on healthcare has quadrupled since 1970 and it could double again by the year 2005. People in the 20-50 year age group average only 4 drug prescriptions per year. Those over 65-years of age have 12 prescriptions filled annually. This "graying of Canada" ensures fast growth for the pharmaceutical sector and some of the best jobs are:

- Bacteriologists
- Biologists
- Chemists
- Embryologists
- Marketing Analysts
- Neurologists
- Sales Representatives

- Biochemists
- Chemical Engineers
- Commercial Travellers
- Lab. Researchers
- Mechanical Engineers
- Production Assemblers
- Toxicologists

New Materials
Everyone knows that plastic continues to replace metal in automobiles and other heavy equipment. The Japanese are convinced they can make an entire car out of ceramics, including the engine block. Ceramics tougher than steel are made from sand, the most common material on Earth. (Silicon chips, also made from sand, are what is driving the micro-electronics revolution). Ceramic parts will replace metal—and plastics—in thousands of products and articles ranging from auto engines to microwave ovens, fuel cells, and parts of the human body.

Other "new materials" research activity is concentrated in the 6th-Wave Outer-Space sector. Materials and structures are a vital part of the development of advanced flight vehicles and the NASA Space Station in which Canada is playing a role. The jobs being created in this field include:

- Aerospace Engineers
- Ceramic Engineers

- Chemists
- Computer Scientists
- Materials Scientists
- Metallurgists
- Physics/Welding Engineers
- Composite Materials Scientists
- Geologists
- Mechanics/Engineers
- Physicists

Radiation/Laser Technologies
Almost daily, new applications are being found for lasers (meaning *Light Amplification by Stimulated Emission of Radiation*) in medicine, energy, industry, computers, communications, entertainment, and outer space.

With mass production, the price of lasers is dropping fast and their use expanding. Lasers are expected to be as important to the 21st century as was electricity to the 20th. They are eliminating many jobs such as machinists, tool-and-die makers, millwrights and sheet metal workers. But in their place are laser technicians—about 150,000 of them in Canada by the year 2005—trained in electro-optics. And they'll earn 30% more than today's welders.

Laser-related jobs are among the fastest-growing job fields. Most large electronics firms employ people trained to plan for, purchase, install, test, operate and maintain laser equipment. Eventually, small shops and mini-factories will have laser equipment, and travelling repairpersons will use portable laser tools. Jobs being created include:

- Laser Beam Welder
- Laser Scientists
- Production Assemblers
- Laser Mechanics
- Laser Surgeons/Therapists
- Radiology Therapists

5th-Wave Careers:

Best Prospects in
Leisure & Tourism

In many ways, we are succeeding magnificently at putting ourselves out of work. We're racing—at electronic speed—towards the "leisure society" that we have craved for the last 2000 years. Early in the next century, Canada will be a 5th-Wave Leisure Society and the fast-growing leisure industry already offers a wide-range of fast-track careers.

Business Week magazine recently calculated that the entertainment and recreation industries added 200,000 workers in 1993 in the United States—a stunning 12% of all net new jobs and more than were hired by the booming healthcare industry. The leisure sector already supplies 23% of Canada's jobs—almost double the 12% in the fast-declining manufacturing sector. Indeed, the leisure sector is the fastest-growing part of the Canadian economy in terms of job-creation and will be the biggest employer by the year 2000. This sector already is the second largest industry (after financial services) in Metro Toronto.

Canadians spent $82-billion in 1993 on recreation, education, and on personal goods and services such as restaurants and hotels—a fourteen-fold increase over 1970. As a proportion of consumer spending, this has increased from 19% to more than 28%. The trend will likely continue. For example, almost 50-cents of every dollar that Canadians spend on food is spent in restaurants. Dining out or bringing home take-out food is now a staple, not a treat. It used to be that one meal out per week was the family treat. Now one family meal at home on the weekend is the family treat.

By the year 2000, as much as 40% of total disposable income will be spent on living a leisureful life—a mammoth $1-trillion. None of these figures include food snacks, soft drinks, booze or smokes, or money spent on lottery tickets and gambling.

In 1993, we spent $19-billion in restaurants and hotels, $13-billion on recreation, sporting and camping equipment, and $9-billion on education and cultural services. The $5-billion spent today on laundry, dry-cleaning, domestic and other household services was 80% of what we spent in *all* "leisure society" categories back in 1965.

Leisure is clearly no longer just for the affluent, the lazy, and the retired (who had "earned" it). Let's review the major sectors of the leisure economy and discover where the best careers are and will be.

Travel & Tourism Industry
Hospitality will be the major growth industry of the late-1990s. There was a slowdown in travel during the "Mini-Depression" (1989-1992) because organizations and individuals always cut back spending in this area during tough economic times. However, by 1993 (as noted above) the industry resumed fast-track growth, creating thousands of jobs.

Although airlines struggled to survive, the demand for flight attendants has been unabated. Due to the high turnover in this profession coming out of the "Mini-Depression," the number of flight attendants is growing rapidly and could soar by 5% a year. If gambling casinos sprout up across Canada, leisure-sector employment could soar even farther. For example, the MGM Grand in Las Vegas alone employs 8,000 people, from croupiers to cocktail waitresses. Overall, the greatest growth in this sector is occurring in the following fields:
- Airline/Cruise Personnel - Airline Pilots/Crew
- Airport Personnel   - Campground Managers
- Car Rental Personnel   - Convention Centre Personnel
- Convention Planners   - Croupiers

- Entertainers
- Group Sales Mgrs/Reps
- Hotel/Resort Operators
- Incentive Travel Experts
- Language Instructors
- Marina Managers
- Park Planners
- Party Planners
- RV Rental Agents
- Reservations Advisors
- Theme Park Personnel
- Tour Bus Guides
- Tourism Policy Analysts
- Travel Agency Mgrs
- Travel Journalists

- Gambling Casino Employees
- Guides
- Hotel/Resort Staff
- Interpreters
- Lottery Ticket Sellers
- Marketers
- Park Supervisors
- Promotion/PR Experts
- Research/Statistical Specialists
- Taxi Drivers
- Ticket Collectors
- Tourism Planners
- Tour Operators
- Travel Agents
- Ushers

Aside from jobs created directly in the tourism industry, of course, there is much indirect job-creation in other sectors: makers of cameras and films, film developers, map makers, service stations, telecom services, education and training, computer vendors, airplane makers, financial services, advertizing agencies, etc.

Food and Beverage Industry
As mentioned, growing numbers of people prefer eating out to cooking in, and the food service industry will continue to boom. While many might think of this industry as being part of the 3rd-Wave Service Economy, the fast-food industry is actually in the business of selling time and convenience; it is in the leisure sector of the economy. And it is growing so fast that there is a huge demand for people to work in this sector.

On the other hand, the fast-food chains are testing robotized cooking and central kitchens which serve groups of nearby restaurants. Laser cookers could eliminate 80% of fast-food jobs during the next few years. This could be the beginning of the end for the so-called hamburger-flipping "McJobs."

Still, with fewer mothers spending time in the kitchen, small bakery shops are opening everywhere—in supermarkets, hotels, and as stand-alone outlets. Other jobs are to be found in catering firms, clubs, bars, hotels/motels, resorts, restaurants and rest homes, as well as in school, office, factory and hospital cafeterias, as follows:

- Bakers   - Baking Technologists
- Bartenders   - Bus Boys/Girls
- Chefs   - Cooks
- Dieticians   - Food and Beverage Managers
- Food Directors   - Food Order Takers
- Food Servers (Waiters)   - Food Technologists
- Gourmet Food Caterers   - Kitchen Staff
- Food Facility Specialists   - Nutritionists
- Restauranteurs   - Restaurant Personnel
- Robot Supervisors

Recreation & Amateur/Professional Sports

There continues to be a growing public interest in health, fitness and recreational activities. However, the aging of the population is causing shifts in emphasis from one activity to another, say from jogging to walking or from baseball to golf. In addition, as people age they tend to become much more oriented towards spectator sports rather than self-participation.

Hence, careers in this entire area should be selected with these trends in mind. Overall, however, this sector of the leisure economy will continue to boom through the late-1990s and there is a large demand for career professionals in the following areas:

- Announcers   - Athletes
- Camp Operators   - Career Camp Counsellors
- Compu-Camp Supervsrs   - Fitness Instructors
- Golf Course Operatives   - Journalists
- Mechanics   - Medical Personnel
- Nurses   - Nutritionists
- Park Planners/Supervsrs   - Physiotherapists

- Promotionalists
- Recreationists
- Scouts
- Sports Coaches
- Sports Psychologists
- Team Managers
- Trainers

- Recreation Centre Managers
- Scorers
- Sportscasters
- Sports Complex Managers
- Statisticians
- Therapists
- Umpires/Officials

Arts & Culture Industry

Despite the growth in sports, the arts are growing even faster and are replacing sports as the primary leisure activity. In 1993, North Americans spent $5-billion attending arts festivals compared with $4-billion for sporting events. Back in 1968, by comparison, sports spending was double the level of arts spending. Increases have occurred across the board: museum attendance doubled between 1965 and 1985; orchestra attendance increased 2½-times between 1965 and 1988; live theatre is now so strong that the *Broadway Theatre* in New York City sells more tickets than the *Yankees* and *Mets* baseball teams combined. In Toronto, the concert halls and theatres next to the *SkyDome* sell more tickets than does the stadium for *Blue Jays* games—which are always sold out.

The arts and culture phenomenon is not restricted to the big cities: local galleries, museums, orchestras and theatres are starting up all across the continent. These trends are very strong in both the U.S. and Canada, and will grow stronger during the late-1990s. This will create a multitude of career opportunities in fields typically thought of as overcrowded and underpaid. The biggest demand is for:

- Actors/Actresses
- Archivists
- Arrangers
- Composers
- Conservators
- Designers
- Electronic Artists

- Agents
- Artists
- Choreographers
- Conductors
- Dancers
- Directors
- Historians

- Impresarios
- Marketing/Sales Experts
- Musicians
- Promoters/Publicists
- Stage Managers

- Lighting Technicians
- Museum/Art Gallery Mgrs
- Playwrights
- Singers

Radio, Television, Videos & Movies

Television has not, as many predicted it would, killed either radio or the movies. On the contrary, each of the media fills a particular market niche. This media specialization and fragmentation will continue. National radio and TV broadcasting are being supplemented and, to a large degree, replaced by local and specialized broadcasting—sometimes called "narrowcasting"—with stations sprouting up rapidly.

In 1993, 12,000 Canadians worked in the studios and offices of, or were hooking up cable subscribers for, local TV broadcasters. The spread of local radio, television, cable and home videos, plus the revival of Hollywood movies, will continue. The major Hollywood studios will produce 198 films in 1994, up 10% from 1993. For its part, Canada has a strong reputation as a place to make movies, and Toronto, Vancouver and Montréal will continue to be used frequently as production sites. These trends are creating a demand for the following "glamour" career aspirants:

- Account Executives
- Administrators
- Camera Operators
- Critics
- Editors
- Entertainment Lawyers
- Lighting Technicians
- News Writers/Editors
- Producers
- Props Personnel
- Researchers
- Screenwriters

- Actors/Actresses
- Agents
- Costumiers
- Directors
- Engineers
- Extras
- Marketing Personnel
- On-Camera Stars
- Program Planners
- Publicists
- Satellite Dish Technicians
- Set Designers

- Set Dressers   - Sound Technicians/Mixers
- Video Engineers

Fashion & Beautycare
The fashion and beauty industry has long suffered from oversupply. For example, there are far too many men's barbers shops and women's hairdressing salons. However, more and more people have more and more time to pamper and glamourize themselves. Also, the middle-aging Baby Boomers and their aging parents want to try to stay looking young and beautiful. There is an increasing demand for "high-touch" beauty care providers and other professionals such as:
- Beauty Consultants   - Cosmetic Surgeons
- Cosmetologists   - Custom Dressmakers
- Custom Tailors   - Dermatologists
- Fashion Designers   - Fashion Merchandisers
- Fashion Models   - Fashion Photographers
- Hairstylers (no Barbers) - Image Consultants
- Lifestyle Marketers   - Manicurists
- Portrait Photographers - Salon Managers
- Stylists

Interior & Exterior Design
As the Baby Boom generation ages, people are tending to spend more time at home with their own families. The lure of hearth and home is an escape from the high-pressured life of the rat-race they led during the 1980s. Marketers call this phenomenon "cocooning" and it is creating a renewed interest in making the home more comfortable, both inside and out.

The trend is reinforced by the increase in the number of people who work from their homes and who want to create more ambient work surroundings. Through the late-1990s, people also will increasingly create entertainment centres inside their homes, decorating their homes in unique ways to reflect their individuality—and doing the same thing in their front and

back yards. This creates a demand for people providing interior design/decorating and exterior landscaping services:
- Drapers
- Floral Designers
- Grounds Keepers
- Interior Decorators
- Interior Designers
- Landscape Gardeners
- Garden Nursery Workers

Pet Care
There is more money spent on pet food in North America than on baby food. Pets are a form of entertainment and leisure and their population is booming as lonely senior citizens buy companions. In addition, pet owners now visit vets twice as often as they did ten years ago. These trends increase demands for:
- Pet Groomers
- Pet Store Assistants
- Veterinarians
- Veterinarian Aides

6th-Wave Careers:

Best Prospects in
The Outer-Space Industry

Almost all high-tech fields of development (discussed in the 4th-Wave section) are brought to a point of focus in the aerospace industry. It is here that almost all leading-edge research and application first occurs.

Most of this activity, of course, occurs in the United States. In 1959, NASA's budget was a mere US$330-million; today it is US$18-billion. Frequent shuttle missions and the commitment to develop and launch a permanently manned space station will further boost career openings and spin-off benefits into the economy at large. The program has three stages:

- Placing the space station in low Earth orbit sending payloads to it on the space shuttle;
- Constructing orbital structures and bases for later use as power stations and further exploration; and
- Exploring the Moon for energy and materials, establishing a mining base, setting up "factories" and building space colonies.

Even without this ambitious program, the world is constantly being encircled with new satellites, the "tom-tom drums" of the Global Village. This space-based info-structure is again transforming all 5-Waves of the Earth-bound economy, revolutionizing farming, mining, telecoms, education, healthcare and various other elements of our everyday lives—and creating thousands of jobs in the process.

Canada is a leader in satellite and communications technologies and is playing a small but meaningful part in the space station program through the Canadian Space Centre in Montréal. Despite budget cutbacks for 1994, this will open up hundreds of additional aerospace careers in Canada during the late-1990s:

- Air-Con Experts	- Astronauts/Crew Members
- Astronomy Technicians	- Astro-Scientists/Aeronomist
- Avionics Engineers	- Biomedical Professionals
- Biotechnologists	- Chemists
- Communications Mgrs.	- Computer Professionals
- Crew Station Designers	- Ecologists
- Equipment Technicians	- Facilities Personnel
- Fitness Experts	- Flight Management Personnel
- Flight Specialists	- Fluid/Flight Mechanics
- Fluid/Flow Technicians	- Food Technologists
- Geodetic Surveyors	- Geologists
- Human Researchers	- Instrumentation Designers
- Laser Engineers	- Launch/Flight Operators
- Life Scientists	- New Materials Engineers
- Nutritionists	- Pharmaceutical Researchers

- Propulsion Engineers
- Psychologists
- Land-Vehicle Engineers
- Roboticists
- Satellite Designers
- Simulator Specialists
- Superconductn. Experts
- Psychiatrists
- Recreationists
- Remote Sensing Data Analysts
- Satellite Antenna Installers
- Shuttle Support Personnel
- Space Applications Scientists
- Telecom/Telemetry Specialists

Section C

BEST CAREERS
Ranked Forecasts for 1995-2005

This section is the "bottom line" on tomorrow's best careers.

To help you get a proper handle on which jobs really offer the best growth prospects, this section provides various tables which rank almost 200 Canadian careers for the late-1990s as follows:

- 90 BEST GROWTH Careers;
- 30 "SO-SO" Jobs;
- 36 BEST PAYING Careers;
- 30 DECLINING Jobs; and
- 36 "DODO" Jobs (the dodo is an extinct bird).

This section also provides a **province-by-province** regional overview of career prospects.

The Job Tables Explained

All jobs are ranked according to their projected percentage growth between 1994 and 2005. Also shown in the rankings are the following pieces of information:

- The % of each job type that will be *held by women* in 2005. Comparisons are not shown with 1994 but women will gain in almost every occupation.

- The % of each job category that will be *part-time*. With a leisure society evolving, more and more jobs will become part-time in most categories. There are some exceptions where part-time jobs are becoming full-time in order to keep up with demand but, by and large, we are becoming a nation of part-time workers. These percentages will help guide those who prefer part-time work.

- The approximate comparative *salary levels* of each career is shown in the "Earnings" column; the more "$" signs, the higher the earnings level vis-a-vis other jobs.

- An assessment of the *stress level* of the job as shown by the symbol "!"; the more exclamation marks, the higher the stress level!

- *Minimum education* requirements for entry level positions are indicated as follows:
    High = High School Diploma;
    Coll = Community College or
                Vocational/Apprenticeship Diploma;
    Univ = University Undergraduate Degree or higher.

- Where on-the-job *travel* is involved, whether to worksites or by car or airplane, this is shown by the letter "T"; the more "Ts," the more travel-intensive the job.

The 90 BEST GROWTH CAREERS to 2005

(Ranked by % growth, 1994-2005)

THE "TOP 30"

Type of Occupation	%Inc over 1994	% Fe- male	% Part Time	Earn- ings ($)	Stress Level (!)	Edu- ca- tion	Job Travel (T)
1 Physician/Surgeon	71	40	15	$$$$	!!!	Univ	
2 Psychiatrist/-ologist	66	50	20	$$$$	!!	Univ	
3 Pharmacist	64	70	30	$$$	!	Univ	
4 Lawyer	62	40	5	$$$$	!!	Univ	TT
5 Nurse	62	90	60	$$	!!!!	Univ	T
6 Vocational Teacher	62	60	25	$$	!	Univ	
7 Osteopath/Chiropractr	61	40	10	$$$$	!	Univ	
8 Nursing Assistant	61	90	70	$	!	Coll	
9 Accountant/Auditor	58	60	25	$$$$	!!	Univ	TT
10 Health Manager	58	60	5	$$$	!!!	Coll	
11 Dispensing Optician	56	70	10	$$	!	Coll	
12 Guidance Counsellor	55	75	20	$$$	!	Univ	T
13 Computer Programr	54	40	15	$$$	!!	Coll	
14 Audio/Physiotherpst	54	90	40	$$	!	Univ	
15 Food/Drink Server	53	90	80	$	!!!!!	High	
16 Radiology Technician	50	90	40	$	!!	Coll	
17 Hospital Orderly	49	80	60	$	!!!	High	
18 Air Pilot/Navigator	49	10	5	$$$$	!!!!	Coll	TTT
19 Food/Drink Sprvsr	49	70	35	$$	!!	Coll	
20 Socio-Anthropologist	48	55	30	$$$$	!	Univ	
21 Dentist/Orthodontist	47	25	10	$$$$	!!	Univ	
22 Dietician/Nutritionist	47	90	40	$$	!	Univ	T
23 Personnel Officer	46	70	15	$$	!	Univ	TT
24 Executive/Snr Offcl	45	40	5	$$$$	!!!!	Univ	TTT
25 Optometrist	44	60	10	$$$$	!	Univ	
26 Veterinarian	44	40	20	$$$$	!!	Univ	TT
27 Denturist/Hygienist	44	95	40	$	!!	Coll	
28 Bus/Transit Driver	44	50	40	$	!!	—	TTT
29 University Professor	43	50	25	$$$$	!	Univ	T
30 Biologist/Bioscientist	43	40	10	$$$	!	Univ	T

The 90 Best Growth Careers to 2005
(Ranked by % growth, 1994-2005)

"Next-Best 30"

# Type of Occupation	%Inc over 1994	% Fe- male	% Part Time	Earn- ings ($)	Stress Level (!)	Edu- ca- tion	Job Travel (T)
31 Telecom Installer	42	10	20	$$	!	Coll	TTT
32 Services Manager	42	45	10	$$	!!	Coll	
33 Product/Intrr Designer	42	90	50	$$	!	Coll	TT
34 Community Planner	41	10	10	$$$	!	Univ	TT
35 Stockbroker/Trader	40	35	10	$$$$	!!!!!	Univ	
36 Special Ed Teacher	40	80	25	$$	!!	Univ	T
37 Travel Attendant	40	80	20	$$	!!!!!	High	TTT
38 Audio-Video Techncn	40	20	15	$	!!!	Coll	
39 Sports/Recrtn. Trainer	38	40	50	$	!!!	Coll	TTT
40 Social Worker	37	70	30	$$	!!!	Univ	TT
41 Medical Lab Techncn	36	90	30	$	!!	Coll	
42 Cleaner/Homecare Aid	36	50	50	$	!!!	—	T
43 Social Service Worker	34	70	30	$	!!!!!	Coll	TT
44 Personnel Manager	33	50	5	$$$$	!!!	Univ	TT
45 Aerospace Engineer	32	10	5	$$$	!	Univ	T
46 TV/Radio/Film Prodcr	32	40	15	$$	!!!!!	Coll	TTT
47 Social Science Mngr	32	60	15	$$	!	Univ	
48 Radio/TV Announcer	32	40	40	$$	!!	Coll	T
49 Sales Supervisor	31	50	15	$$$	!!	Coll	TTT
50 Painter/Paperhanger	31	5	40	$	!	—	T
51 Financial Comptroller	30	50	5	$$$$	!!	Univ	T
52 Transportation Mgr	30	10	5	$$$$	!!	Coll	TT
53 Secondy Schl Teacher	30	55	25	$$	!!!	Univ	T
54 PR Officer/Agent	30	60	20	$$	!!!!	Univ	TTT
55 Librarian/Curator	30	60	25	$	!	Univ	
56 Photographer/Grip	30	30	40	$	!!	High	TT
57 Garden/Nursery Staff	30	30	40	$	!	High	TTT
58 Salesperson	29	70	60	$	!!	High	
59 Radio/TV Stn Techncn	28	30	20	$	!!	High	T
60 Air Traffic Controller	28	10	5	$$$$	!!!!!	High	

The 90 Best Growth Careers to 2005
(Ranked by % growth, 1994-2005)

"Third-Best 30"

# Type of Occupation	%Inc over 1994	% Fe-male	% Part Time	Earn-ings ($)	Stress Level (!)	Edu-ca-tion	Job Travel (T)
61 Translator/Interpreter	27	60	40	$$	!!!!!	Univ	TTT
62 Techncl Sales/Advisor	26	15	10	$$$	!!	Coll	TT
63 EDP Operator	26	80	10	$$	!!!	High	
64 Artist/Illustrator	26	40	30	$	!!	Coll	T
65 Musician/Singer	26	35	40	$	!!!	Coll	TT
66 Education Managers	25	35	10	$$$	!!	Univ	T
67 Police Offcr/Detective	25	20	10	$$	!!!	Coll	TTT
68 Security Guard	25	30	50	$	!!	—	TT
69 Photograph Processor	25	70	25	$	!	Coll	
70 Actor/Actress	25	50	60	$	!!!!!	Coll	TTT
71 Receptnst/Info Clerk	24	95	50	$	!!	High	
72 Writer/Editor	24	50	60	$	!!!	Univ	TT
73 Secretary/Steno	24	99	40	$	!!!!!	Coll	
74 K-7 Elementy Teacher	23	90	25	$$	!!!	Univ	T
75 Insurance Salesperson	21	20	30	$$	!!!	Coll	T
76 Chef/Cook	21	40	70	$	!!!!	Coll	
77 Advertizing Manager	20	30	10	$$$	!!	Coll	TT
78 Advertzg/Sales Expert	20	60	20	$$	!!	Coll	T
79 Inspector (Govt.)	20	5	5	$$	!	Coll	TT
80 Forester/Eco-Scientist	20	20	5	$$	!	Coll	T
81 Choreographer/Dancer	20	80	40	$	!!!!	Coll	TT
82 Sales Supervisor	19	40	10	$$$	!!	Coll	TT
83 Archivist/Conservator	19	75	40	$$	!!	Univ	
84 Travel Agent/Clerk	18	80	40	$$	!!!!	High	TTT
85 Realty Salesperson	18	60	40	$$	!!	High	TT
86 Drafter/Designer	18	30	10	$$	!	Coll	T
87 Physicist	17	15	5	$$$	!	Univ	T
88 Architect	17	10	10	$$$	!	Univ	TT
89 Construction Manager	15	1	5	$$$	!!	Coll	TT
90 Geologist	15	5	5	$$$	!	Univ	TTT

30 "SO-SO" JOBS in CANADA to 2005
(Ranked by % growth, 1994-2005)

# Type of Occupation	%Inc over 1994	% Fe- male	% Part Time	Earn- ings ($)	Stress Level (!)	Edu- ca- tion	Job Travel (T)
91 Electrical Engineer	15	5	10	$$$	!!	Univ	T
92 Forestry Technician	15	25	5	$$	!	Coll	TTT
93 Business Servicer	15	50	20	$$	!!	Coll	TTT
94 Equipment Installer	15	20	20	$	!!	Coll	TTT
95 Civil Engineer	14	5	5	$$$	!	Univ	TT
96 Inspector (non-Govt)	14	5	10	$$	!	Coll	TTT
97 Insurance Adjuster	14	20	25	$$	!	High	TTT
98 Commercl Traveller	13	15	15	$$$	!!!	Coll	TTT
99 Science Manager	12	5	5	$$$	!	Univ	
100 EDP Supervisor	11	40	10	$$	!!!	Coll	
101 Equipment Tester	11	10	10	$$	!!	Coll	T
102 Fire-Fighter	10	—	20	$$	!!	High	TT
103 Funeral Director	10	5	10	$$	!	Coll	T
104 Metals Tester	8	—	10	$	!	Coll	
105 Auto Mechanic	8	5	25	$	!	Coll	
106 Brick/Tile Layer	8	—	10	$	!	High	TT
107 Concrete Finisher	7	—	10	$	!	—	TT
108 Plasterer/Dry-Waller	5	—	25	$	!	—	TT
109 Roofer/Waterproofer	6	—	30	$	!!!	—	TT
110 Industrial Engineer	5	—	5	$$	!	Univ	
111 Architect Techncn	5	—	—	$	!	Coll	TT
112 Glazier	3	—	20	$	!!!	—	TT
113 Carpenter/Woodwrkr	3	—	10	$	!	Coll	TT
114 Chemist	3	30	—	$$$	!	Univ	
115 Economist	3	40	—	$$$	!	Univ	
116 Production Manager	2	5	10	$$	!!	Coll	
117 Hairdstyler/Beauticn	2	80	65	$	!	High	
118 General Office Clerk	2	80	80	$	!!!	High	
119 Cashier/Teller	1	90	70	$	!!!	High	
120 Typist/Clerk-Typist	1	95	70	$	!!!!!	High	

The BEST PAYING JOBS in CANADA to 2005
(Ranked by % growth, 1994-2005)

The "BIG BUCK 36"

# Type of Occupation	%Inc over 1994	% Fe-male	% Part Time	Earn-ings ($)	Stress Level (!)	Edu-ca-tion	Job Travel (T)
1 Physician/Surgeon	71	40	15	$$$$	!!!	Univ	
2 Psychiatrist/-ologist	66	50	20	$$$$	!!	Univ	
3 Pharmacist	64	70	30	$$$	!	Univ	
4 Lawyer	62	40	5	$$$$	!!	Univ	TTT
7 Osteopath/Chiropractr	61	40	10	$$$$	!	Univ	
9 Accntnt/Auditor	58	60	25	$$$$	!!	Univ	TT
10 Health Administrator	58	60	5	$$$	!!!	Univ	
12 Guidance Counsellor	55	75	20	$$$	!	Univ	T
13 Computer Programr	54	40	15	$$$	!!	Coll	
18 Air Pilot/Navigator	49	10	5	$$$$	!!!!	Coll	TTT
20 Socio-Anthropologist	48	55	30	$$$$	!	Univ	
21 Dentist/Orthodontist	47	25	10	$$$$	!!	Univ	
24 Executive/Snr Offcl	45	40	5	$$$$	!!!!	Univ	TTT
25 Optometrist	44	60	10	$$$$	!	Univ	
26 Veterinarian	44	40	20	$$$$	!!	Univ	TT
29 University Professor	43	50	25	$$$$	!	Univ	T
34 Community Planner	41	10	10	$$$	!	Univ	TT
35 Stockbroker/Trader	40	35	10	$$$$	!!!!!	Univ	
44 Personnel Manager	33	50	5	$$$$	!!!	Univ	TT
45 Aerospace Engineer	32	10	5	$$$	!	Univ	T
49 Sales Supervisor	31	50	15	$$$	!!	Coll	TTT
51 Financial Comptroller	30	50	5	$$$$	!!	Univ	T
52 Transportation Mgr	30	10	5	$$$$	!!	Coll	TT
62 Techncl Sales/Advisor	26	15	10	$$$	!!	Coll	TT
66 Education Manager	25	35	10	$$$	!!	Univ	T
77 Advertizing Manager	20	30	10	$$$	!!	Coll	TT
87 Physicist	17	15	5	$$$$	!	Univ	T
88 Architect	17	10	10	$$$	!	Univ	TT
89 Construction Manager	15	1	5	$$$	!!	Coll	TT
90 Geologist	15	5	5	$$$$	!	Univ	TTT
91 Electrical Engineer	15	5	10	$$$	!!	Univ	T
95 Civil Engineer	14	5	5	$$$	!	Univ	TT
98 Commercial Traveller	13	15	15	$$$	!!!	Coll	TTT
99 Science Manager	12	5	5	$$$$	!	Univ	
114 Chemist	3	30	—	$$$	!	Univ	
115 Economist	3	40	—	$$$	!	Univ	

Where Canada's Best Jobs Will Be:
Provincial ... Local ... Global

Provincial Job Prospects

As discussed in Section A, the six waves of the economy manifest themselves in varying strengths and speeds in different countries and regions. Manitoba, Saskatchewan and Alberta, for example, are mainly 1st-Wave economies. Yet, even there, economic diversification means that most of the jobs are in the 2nd-, 3rd-, 4th-, and 5th-Wave sectors. As the new waves pile on top of the previous ones, they build the economy and enhance human development. But the fortunes of individual provinces vary depending on their drive to change, on their degree of innovation, and on other constraints and opportunities.

Québec

Québec nationalists are in great danger of isolating the province from the North American and global marketplace. Fortunately, Québec's growing entrepreneurial class recognizes—if some of its politicians do not—that the global *lingua franca* (language of daily use) is English. They also have embraced the opportunities of NAFTA. The future economic success of this class represents Québec's best chance to overcome its fear of cultural assimilation, allowing it to prosper.

The language issue also balkanizes Canada at large, saps its social energy, and weakens economic progress. If the next generation of Québécois can reach a higher level of political maturity and overcome their irrational assimilation fears, the province—and Canada—will be more likely to achieve its larger potential. For this to happen, Québec must be re-Canadianized—within the larger North American and global context. Once this occurs, Québec will prosper and career growth will resurge.

Atlantic Canada

Isolated from the rest of Canada by Québec, the Atlantic Provinces are closer—socially (due to family ties) and economically (due to trade and tourism)—to the New England states of America. This proximity, however, hasn't made these provinces affluent. Thanks to the conditioning of Canadian federal government aid over several decades, these provinces are trapped in a social welfare mentality (unemployment in Newfoundland is perennially around 15% even in the best of times) which now expects federal aid as a birthright.

The provinces have mainly failed to diversify out of, or to modernize, a distinctly stagnant 1st-Wave fishing industry and are economically backward. New Brunswick has done the best job of economic diversification, attracting a number of telecom and computer service industries. Beyond that, Atlantic Canada's best prospect is to further develop the tourism sector, drawing on the huge New England and New York markets. Overall, career prospects are poor in the entire region.

Prairies

Canada's prairie provinces also have strong north-south links with the American mid-West. Like the American mid-West, however, Manitoba and Saskatchewan have not yet sufficiently diversified out of their globally noncompetitive, 1st-Wave agricultural economy. And, like Texas, Alberta has counted too much on an oil bonanza that will never return.

Still, these provinces are reasonably self-sufficient and record steady if unspectacular economic progress even in the worst of times. They also are gradually realizing that they are no longer the "bread basket" of the world and are slowly developing new industries that hold better potential. Alberta also is becoming a leading centre of tourism for jet-setting Japanese and the rapidly-growing city populations of the U.S. northwest that are drawn to the breathtaking Alberta scenery in the Rocky Mountains. For this reason, of the three Prairie provinces, Alberta offers the best—but not spectacular—career prospects.

British Columbia

Psychologically cut off from Canada by the same Rocky Mountains, BC is capitalizing on the economic vibrancy of the Pacific Rim. But its progress is being negated by a social malaise of labour strife and a prevailing 1st-Wave forest industry mentality that is causing the province to fall further behind the post-industrial world. In comparison with the neighbouring American states of Washington and Oregon, for example, BC clearly is not keeping pace, either in developing its high-tech or its Pacific potentials.

Still, information technology will soon pass mining to become BC's third-largest industry after forestry and tourism. Vancouver also is strategically located and ought to be able to play a full part in the booming American northwest and Pacific Rim economies during the next half-century. Strong growth will continue in the lower mainland, with the best career prospects being in the Greater Vancouver area which will be second only to the Greater Toronto Area in economic growth.

Ontario

Almost 40% of Canada's economy and its jobs are accounted for by Ontario. As economically strong, as vibrant, as innovative, and as high-tech as California, Ontario is the centre of economic gravity in Canada and the undoubted epicentre of Canada's future post-industrial efforts. Toronto, the Baby Boom capital of Canada, is the nation's corporate headquarters and its centre of finance, media and information.

Ontario is the country's leader in high technology and a major North American tourism centre. While not located on the Pacific Rim, Ontario has a growing trade with Southeast Asia and other parts of the developing world, and its overall prospects are spectacular. The very best career prospects in all of Canada will be found in southern Ontario, particularly the golden horseshoe area centred on Toronto.

Local Career Prospects

While most Canadian jobs are in our major cities, work is also being decentralized away from urban centres. Escalating home prices, high commercial property rents, and an aversion to city congestion will continue to cause many service-related companies and departments to move from inner cities and suburbs to the exurbs—smaller towns up to 100-miles from major downtown areas. This trend is especially evident near Toronto and, to a certain extent, Montreal and Vancouver.

Suburbs are growing into large independent satellite cities that now rival and even surpass the old downtown core as the centre of economic power and vitality. In the Greater Toronto Area (GTA), for example, outer cities such as Mississauga, North York and Scarborough have become major urban entities all of their own. Evolving landscapes of skyscrapers, office parks, and retail palaces create a sense of "downtown" in the suburban sprawl. It is in these outer cities where employment is now being generated, and where labour shortages exist.

Such urban decentralization is a natural aspect of the 4th-Wave economy. The first real surge of city growth occurred 100-years ago, with the onset of the Industrial Revolution. With the arrival of the automobile, cities mushroomed again. The personal computer reverses this process: information workers do not need to travel to work in the downtown core; now the work can travel to them, electronically.

Regional and national headquarters of big companies are even moving to the suburbs, as are hotels, restaurants, and such specialized functions as banking, accounting services and legal offices, once thought to be geographically immovable bastions of downtown enterprise. The evolution is towards more urban amenities in the outer cities which, once all the elements are put together, spell what a sense of community is all about.

Meanwhile, historic preservation of cultural heritage is providing a new vision for the future of downtown, the central locale of the new major educational, cultural and entertainment assets of society. New historic districts provide a sense of place and history that the outlying centres cannot match. The old downtowns can thus become revitalized gathering places at the centre of a network of decentralized exurban forms, to create an uplifting "super-city" of genuine community spirit—and yet more jobs in the 5th-Wave leisure sector of Canada's economy.

Global Career Prospects

The world at large also offers bright career prospects for Canadians because Canada enjoys an excellent international reputation—for its political impartiality and sensitivity, and its distinctly un-American image—particularly in the Third World. Canada's increasingly multicultural population provides the country with a unique edge in its ability to conduct business around the world. In the late-1990s and beyond, Canadians will be able to look forward to expanded world trade, with thousands of Canadian jobs being created both at home and abroad.

Thanks to NAFTA, Canada will gradually become a full member of a North American ("AMEXICANA") common market. However, this is being achieved at the expense of expanding ties in the Third World—especially Asia. In the long run, such ties will be much more economically fruitful for Canada than will those with the United States.

In general, of course, Canada's future prosperity—within NAFTA or the world—essentially rests on its ability to export modern technology, expertise and information. The country which developed the telephone is now re-inventing the phone and is a world leader in integrated services digital network (ISDN) technology. Canada also is a leader in satellite technology and a major participant in the NASA space shuttle and space station programs. Whether or not Canada enhances its technology will determine the appeal of many occupations—and our future well-being as a nation.

If this occurs, many of the best Canadian careers will be *outside* Canada. With the ongoing integration of the world economy and the spread of global corporations—many of them Canadian—thousands of us will find ourselves pursuing careers abroad.

Many exciting possibilities exist for people to develop "global" careers, either with Canadian employers or with big companies who need qualified people.

What the Worst Jobs Will Be:
"Sunset/Sunrise" Industries/Careers

Jobs constantly become outdated and disappear as new technology radically shifts employment from the "sunset" to the "sunrise" industries across the six waves of the economy.

Most of the maturing (and often declining) "sunset" industries are, quite naturally, in the old waves of the economy. However, as the "deadwood" gets pruned from these industries, what remains does show some element of new growth and new career opportunities.

Nevertheless, by far the fastest growth is occurring in the 3rd-, 4th-, and 5th-Wave sectors of the economy. Even there, however, some jobs are being changed or replaced, as the first table on the next page illustrates.

Naturally, on a regional basis, the *worst* career prospects will be in those areas most dependent on old, declining industries: Atlantic Canada and the northern parts of Québec, Ontario and British Columbia.

This is reflected in the subsequent lists of declining and disappearing ("dodo") jobs respectively.

Industrial & Career Restructuring

Wave	"Sunset" Industries/Careers	"Sunrise" Industries/Careers
1st-Wave	Farming, fishing, forestry, mining, fossil fuels (oil, coal).	Biotech farming, aquaculture, environmental restoration, hydro/solar electricity.
2nd-Wave	Textiles/clothing, leather/shoes, steel, metal fabricating, machinery, auto assembly, shipbuilding, railroads, trucking, product assembly, printing, construction, wood products.	Custom-tailored fashions, plastics, ceramics, new materials, light manufacturing, mass/urban transit, aircraft/airports, robotic manufacturing, 3rd/4th/5th-Wave construction.
3rd-Wave	*Business services* (telex/courier/clerical/bookkeeping/typing). *Personal services* painting/plumbing/wallpapering/gas pumps). *Repair services* (TVs/radios/appliances/watches).	*Business services* (fax/accounting/audit/taxation/tele-computer applications). *Personal services* (financial/medical/childcare/eldercare/social services). *Do-it-Yourself retailing*.
4th-Wave	Traditional libraries. Mass education. Keypunch/data input. Computer programs.	Electronic libraries. Individualized learning. Electronic databanks. High-tech services.
5th-Wave	Muscle/fitness clubs. Ticket sellers/agents.	All other leisure/tourism/recreation/entertainment.
6th-Wave	(None)	All Outer-Space industries.

30 Declining Jobs in Canada to 2005
(Approx % decline, 1994-2005)

Type of Occupation	% Decrease	Type of Occupation	% Decrease
Agriculturist/Related Scientist	- 5	Metal Products Inspector	-20
Aircraft Fabricator/Assembler	-10	Metal Forming Inspector	-20
Aircraft Mechanic/Repairer	-10	Petroleum Engineer	-10
Business Machine Repairer	-15	Physical Science Technologist	-10
Chemical Engineer	-10	Power Station Operator	-10
Construction Electrician	- 5	Precision Instrument Mechanic	-15
Excavating/Grading Operative	-10	Purchasing Manager	-10
Constrctn Machine Mechanic	-20	Purchasing Officer	-10
Farm Manager	-15	Shipping & Receiving Clerk	-15
Insulation Installer	-10	Stock Clerk	-20
Insurance/Bank/Fncl Clerk	-10	Structural Metal Erector	-10
Jewellery Fabricator/Repairer	-10	Sundry Mechanics/Repairer	-10
Marine Craft Fabrictr/Repairer	-20	Surveyor	-10
Mechanical Engineer	-10	Tailors & Dressmaker	-10
Metal Machng Inspector	-15	Ticket/Station/Freight Agent	-20

36 Disappearing "DODO" Jobs
(Approx % decline, 1994-2005)

Occupation	% Decrease	Occupation	% Decrease
Blasting Operative	-25	Railroad Equipment Mechanic	-35
Boilermaker/Metal Worker	-30	Rock & Soil Driller	-20
Bookkeeper/Accounting Clerk	-35	Rotary Well-Driller	-20
Furniture Maker/Upholsterer	-25	Sheet Metal Worker	-30
Drill Press Operator	-25	Ship Deck Officer	-35
Farmer	-40	Ship Engineering Officer	-35
Fishermen	-50	Shoemaker/Repairer	-20
Fishing Vessel Captain/Officer	-40	Stationary/Utilities Engineer	-30
Locomotive Operative	-45	Statistical Clerk	-60
Log Inspector/Grader	-40	Telephone Installer	-30
Lumberjack	-25	Telephone Line Installer	-35
Mail & Postal Clerk	-25	Telephone Operator	-35
Metallurgical Engineer	-25	Textile Pattern Maker/Cutter	-30
Mining Engineer	-25	Tool & Die Maker	-30
Molder/Metal Caster	-20	Typesetter/Compositor	-35
Printing Press Operator	-25	Typist (on Typewriter)	-80
Production Clerk	-30	Watch & Clock Repairer	-40
Radio/TV Set Repairer	-30	Welder & Flame Cutter	-25

Section D

Futuristic Career Planning
with Worksheets

It goes without saying that the best jobs will go to those who prepare for them. Future trends challenge all of us to find a new set of lenses through which to manage our careers in the new information economy.

This new perspective requires that you adopt a new mindset about career planning and understand your own personality and what kind of career might best suit you. To help you figure that out, this section covers the following topics:

- Information Age Mindset for Career Planning;
- Open Career Path Flexibility;
- Is It Time to Move On?
- Getting a Fix on Your Future;
- Potential Life Scenario;
- Fixing Your Future;
- Picking a Career to Best Suit Your Personality;
- Personality/Occupation Matching Matrix;
- Choosing the Best Job Function in the Best Career Field;
- Selecting a Preferred Work Pattern;
- Inventing Your Own Career.

Photocopying of Worksheets
and
Bulk Copy Reprints

This section includes many worksheets.

If this book is a library copy,
STUDENTS
may photocopy
ONE SET
of worksheets
(please, only 1 copy for your personal use).

EDUCATORS and GUIDANCE COUNSELLORS
may obtain
bulk copy reprints
of this Section in booklet form
(see back page of book for ordering details).

Information Age Mindset
for Career Planning

A career is a lifetime journey not a day trip. And planning for that journey in the Information Age requires a totally different mindset. The old industrial era way of thinking about a career was to assume that you would follow a fixed career for an entire lifetime, with the same employer, and then retire. Today, one in eight people change their occupation in a given year.

The new information age calls for flexible (not fixed) career goals with several employers (not one), probably switching careers several times, and deciding your own retirement age. The difference between the old- and new-style career is as follows:

Industrial Age Career Mind-Set	Information Age Career Mind-Set
• Plan for fixed and specific life goal.	• Plan for flexible and tentative life goals.
• Find a secure job for life with one specific job skill.	• Develop a broad range of skills to feel secure in a variety of jobs.
• Prepare for a fixed skill.	• Educate yourself continually and lifelong.
• Specialize.	• Be a generalist-specialist.
• Keep up with specific job tasks.	• Keep up with developments in a family of jobs/skills.
• Be a financial success.	• Seek overall life satisfaction.

With an Information Age mind-set, a career also proceeds through different stages of development. As shown on the next page, initial progress is quicker and the career path proceeds more flexibly.

Stages of an Industrial Age Career

Growth Stage (Age 5-13)
Develop picture of your world
and your role in it.
Pursue the work ethic.
Orientation to world of
manual work.

Exploration (Age 14-24)
Pick a job.
Find the job.
Change jobs only if/when
new one is found.

Establishment (Age 25-44)
Consolidate your career
and advance in it.

Do a good job and
climb the ladder.

Maintenance (Age 45-65)
Preserve status and
what you have achieved.

Decline & Fall (Age 65)
Disengage from work.
Retire.
Boredom/death.

Stages of an Info Age Career

Growth Stage (Age 2-10)
Learn a primary base of
information.
Balance work and leisure.
Orientation to world of
brain/knowledge work.

Preparation (Age 11-26)
Plan a lifestyle/career.
Learn multiple skills base.
Enter first job assignment,
switching as needed to
pursue career.

Progression (Age 27-On)
Build on knowledge base,
acquire new skills, keep
up with job market changes
and new career options.
Career self-assessment,
feedback, and decisions to
change if required.
Develop new career goals.

Diversification (No set age)
Implement careers goals.
Establish the right career
path for you.

Non-Retirement (No set age)
Reduce formal career activity.
Start consulting business.
Self-enriching leisure-time.

(Source: Adapted from *Career Tracks* by Schwartz & Brechner; NY, Ballantine, 1985)

Open Career Path Flexibility

The Information Age also provides greater flexibility in selecting a career, or in switching careers throughout life. New career options may be full-time or part-time, with the same or several new employers, or may be totally freelance. The new career path is also likely to involve periods of further education and retraining, or perhaps an internship with another organization, or even a period of leave (a sabbatical) for heavy study or vacation before resuming a career *(as diagrammed below)*.

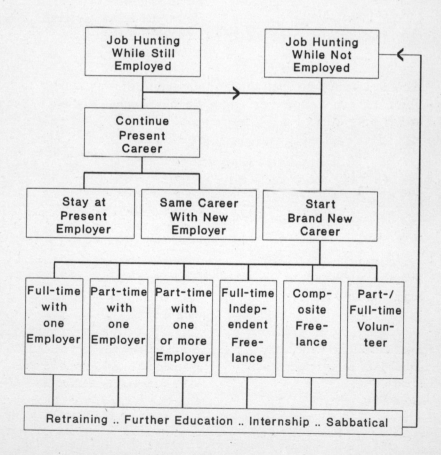

Is it Time to Move On?

How do you decide if or when it's time to make a job or career move? If you are working hard but don't enjoy your job, you likely will develop a poor attitude. That will result in poorer performance and career stagnation. You'll get more discouraged, develop a still worse attitude, become even less conscientious, and your work situation will deteriorate farther.

The time to move on is well before this happens to you. To assess your existing career mindset, simply answer the following set of questions about your work situation and yourself.

My Work Situation

Yes No   Is it more than 3 years since my last promotion?

Yes No   Am I doing more duties for the same pay?

Yes No   Have duties been taken away from me?

Yes No   Is my company uncompetitive in the market?

Yes No   Am I concerned about my job security?

Yes No   Do I feel underpaid?

Yes No   Am I underappreciated?

Yes No   Am I excluded from decision-making?

Yes No   Has work stopped being fun?

My Personal Situation

Yes No   Is my present position keeping me from achieving my career goal?

Yes No   Does my time at work interfere with my personal or family life?

Yes No   Is my job adversely affecting my health?

Yes No   Has a friend, family member, or work colleague suggested that I search for another job?

Yes No   Is my present job/career path detracting from my lifestyle?

Yes No   Do I hate going to work in the morning?

Now, total up your "Yes" answers. Then go to the next page.

If you answered "Yes" to the questions on the previous page:

● **Up to 4 times ...**
Recognize that life is never perfect. Unless you're un-
happy in this job, try to work on those aspects of the job,
work situation, or your own performance that caused you
to answer "Yes."

● **5—9 times ...**
You probably have peaked on this job. You have entered
a transitional period and now is the time to investigate
new career horizons, either inside or outside your existing company.

● **10 or more times ...**
Don't wait another moment to focus on yourself and your
career options. It's definitely time to move on!

Getting a Fix on Your Future

Let's be honest, whatever career you embark upon, the chances
are very high that you will switch jobs and careers more than
once in the future. Aside from your own whim to switch jobs,
the main reason for this is that (as discussed) many of today's
jobs simply will not exist in 10 or 20 years. Moreover, even
some of the new jobs created during the next 10-20 years will
also become obsolete before you decide that your "working"
life is over.

In spite of the potential for rapid job obsolescence in some
fields, it is quite possible to project your own future and plan
your career (or mixture of careers). In fact, the rapid change
in the workplace should aid you to effectively invent and con-
tinuously re-invent your own job. Let me explain.

Before even starting to think about what career you wish to
pursue and which job you'll use as your career launching pad,

it is a good idea to get a fix on your own future in a very specific sense—at least as you now see that future. A good way to get a fix on your future is to "put it down on paper."

To help you appreciate how your own life might change in the future, on the following pages is a scenario of the possible life of someone born in Canada in 1990.

The subsequent blank chart allows you to draw a profile of your own life, at least through to the year 2015. Simply fill in the blanks, starting with your age, and a picture of your life in 2015 will evolve before your eyes—in black and white!

Having done that, you must then decide if you like what you see. What aspects of your life in the year 2015 are you pleased with; what would you like to change? Then re-assess the profile based on what is happening in society at large as outlined at the start of this book.

Potential Life Scenario

One of the Many Alternative Life Cycles
The Future Might Offer

Major Changes in the Life of John Smith: 1990-2100

Age 4-5: Attended elementary school in Toronto.
Age 6-8: Attended elementary school in Vancouver.
Age 9:   Travelled with a class of fifteen students to a number of East Asian countries for six months; Learned some Japanese and Chinese.
Age 10: Returned to Canada and resumed formal studies.
Age 11: Started performing freelance computer work, part-time.
Age 14: Entered rotating work-study "Co-op Ed" program, electing to serve as apprentice in four fields: architecture, social research, computer/communications science, tourism.
Age 17: Went back to formal studies in liberal arts/culture; also took advanced courses in architecture and aerospace.

Age 19:   Spent 3 years abroad, studying comparative architecture in frontier settlements of S.E.Asia.

Age 22:   Returned to Canada and was employed as a computer design draftsman for an international hotel chain; lived for 2 years in an exurban commune with nine other young professionals.

Age 24:   Moved into an apartment with three friends—two female and one male; became "married" to each other, pooling all income and properties.

Age 27:   "Divorced" from living arrangements and married a woman who was also divorced. She had one child, aged 6; took and passed space-architecture exams.

Age 35:   With wife, took two-year leaves from jobs, took 14-year-old son and went to live in Japan; jointly developed interests in the arts: Japanese painting, sketching, sculpting, and electronic painting.

Age 38:   Divorced wife and lived alone.

Age 50:   Set up house with two career women (one Filipino, one Australian) in their late-30s; the relationship was economic and sexual, but not exclusive.

Age 60:   Left job and residence; went to teach advanced communications science to students in central China.

Age 65:   Returned to Canada and resumed work part-time, travelling between Canada, U.S. and Mexico (now called Amexicana); went back to school part-time to update education.

Age 67:   Remarried, to a Chinese woman with 2 children, both grown up with kids of their own.

Age 72:   Took 2-year leave; Travelled around the world with wife and one of the Chinese grandchildren who remained with a family friend in Shanghai; returned to Vancouver.

Age 74:   Resumed work/studies in Shanghai; became interested in laser photography, developing it as hobby and part-time business; Wife died of mysterious new disease.

Age 80:   Took on a teaching position at Fudan University in Shanghai (students ranged in age from 12 to 87 years), lecturing on comparative space architecture.

Age 85:   Consulted to the Third World Space Agency in India on lunar architecture.

Age 92:   Took shuttle flight to Space Station; remarried an Indo-Chinese and settled in the Philippines; consulted on satellite education system for remote islands.

Age 97:   Completed a book entitled *East Asian Architecture in Outer Space* and lectured internationally on the topic via satellite.

Age 104: Decided to retire and travel the world studying cultures still stuck in obsolete 1990s-type thinking patterns.

Age 109: Died of sudden lung failure while in remote part of India where no transplant donor was available.

Fixing Your Future

Personal Profile Matrix Worksheet				
Characteristic	**2000**	**2005**	**2010**	**2015**
Age in Years				
Parents' Ages				
Reside With ?				
Married/Single				
# of Children				
Where Living				
Education Levels				
Study Interests				
Hobbies				
Occupation(s)				
Annual Income				

Picking a Career to Best Suit Your Personality

Career success also depends on knowledge about yourself. A popular career planning tool that lets you relate your personality to different job types was first developed by John Holland, a vocational psychologist at Johns Hopkins University *(see table on the following pages)*.

From the left-hand column of this table you can identify your strongest interests and determine your basic personality type. You probably will find that your personality overlaps two or three of the six types listed. That's normal.

The next step is to determine your most suitable occupation from among the choices illustrated in the right-hand column. Note that the careers listed are only a sample; this is not a complete list, but rather a selection of jobs that typify each group.

Let us work through a simple example. From the left-hand column you may determine that your personality fits the artistic, investigative and social types in various ways.

If so, you should consider career options such as criminology, journalism and education respectively. In turn, this might lead you to conclude that you should pursue a career in lawcourt journalism or perhaps as a teacher of legal reporting, or some other combination of those areas of expertise most suited to you.

By selecting a career in this way, you are more likely to embark on a career that lets you capitalize on your strengths in a field that most satisfies your personality.

That kind of motivation almost guarantees career success. The job you always wanted *can* be yours. And you'll always have fun doing it.

Personality/Occupation Matching Matrix

Personality

Matching Occupation

Conventional Types:
Data/detail oriented people: conscientious, orderly, and self-controlled.
Prefer: to work with words and numbers, carrying out detailed instructions.
Dislike: ambiguity, unstructured/unsystematic activities.

Assemblers, clerks, bookkeepers, accountants, secretary/stenos, economists, stock brokers, bankers, computer programmers, medical records keepers, fast food servers, court reporters, researchers, stock/order clerks, etc.

Realistic Types:
Technically and athletically inclined: stable, materialistic, frank, self-reliant and practical.
Prefer: to work with hands/ tools to build/repair or grow things, often outdoors.
Dislike: educational or therapeutic activities, self-expression, or working with people and new ideas.

Farmers, foresters, fish and wildlife managers, mechanical engineers, designers and drafters, electronic engineers, landscape gardeners and nursery workers, construction workers, housekeepers, hydro line installers, telephone installers, machine repairers and testers, plumbers, welders, carpenters, etc.

Investigative Types:
Abstract problem solvers: analytical, independent, curious and precise.
Prefer: to work alone, learn, observe, probe, investigate, and solve problems, often in a scientific area.
Dislike: repetitive activity.

Oceanographers, marine biologists, psychiatrists, doctors chemists, economists, engineers, systems analysts, mathematicians, anthropologists, social researchers, medical practitioners, criminologists, police officers, lawyers, etc.

(Continued)

Artistic Types:

Idea creators: imaginative, idealistic, original, intuitive, expressive.
Prefer: to work with their minds—innovating, imagining, creating, designing.
Dislike: structured situations, rules, physical work.

Musicians, artists, actors, actresses, broadcasters, set/interior designers, writers, philosophers, architects, designers, journalists, editors, advertizing professionals, marketers, etc.

Social Types:

People helpers: co-operative and helpful, understanding, tactful, sociable, ethical.
Prefer: working with people; informing, enlightening, helping, training, developing or curing them.
Dislike: machinery and physical exertion.

Nurses, educators, personnel managers, recruiters, training professionals, speech/occupational therapists, nurses, psychologists, social workers, nutritionists, dieticians, sociologists, counsellors, receptionists, etc.

Enterprising Types:

People influencers: persuasive, domineering, energetic, ambitious, flirtatious.
Prefer: to work with people; influencing, leading, organ-, izing, and managing them.
Dislike: precise work, concentrated intellectual work, and systematic activities.

Entrepreneurs, business managers, administrators, hotel/motel managers, real estate professionals, public administrators, retailers, labour leaders, marketers, salespeople, lawyers, public relations experts, etc.

(Adapted from Borchard, Kelly, Weaver, *Your Career: Choices, Chances, Changes*; Kendall/Hunt Publishing; Dubuque, Iowa, 1982)

Choosing the Best Job Function
in the Best Career Field

Don't get stuck with any old job. Jobs and careers can be described as falling either into fields or functions:

● **Job field** relates to the specific industry or profession in which that job or career is to be found (e.g., agriculture, manufacturing, banking, healthcare, tourism);

● **Job function** relates to the type of work that will be carried out (e.g., administration, finance, production, marketing, sales, personnel).

Because job functions cross over all industries and some jobs cross various functions, you should try to find the most suitable "field-function mix" to suit your personality.

For example, administrative jobs are in all industries and may cross various functions in individual firms. Entry-level jobs also may cross functions, especially in a small company where you may get to perform a variety of tasks. In mid-size companies, a departmental secretary may be an office manager and also do bookkeeping.

Also realize that while functions cross the various fields or industries, a marketing job in agriculture will be quite different from one in tourism.

In the opposite matrix, enter those fields (or industries) in the four column sub-headings that most attract you.

Then rate those selections across the various functions, scoring 10 for the most suitable job function and zero for the least attractive.

Job/Career Function	Potential Industry Field (Enter fields and rate 0-10)			
Administration				
Finance				
R & D				
Production				
Marketing				
Sales				
Advertising				
Public Relations				
Personnel				

Based on the scores you have allocated, you now have yet another picture of the career that is most suitable for you.

Selecting a Preferred Work Pattern

In planning your career, you should think about:
- how many hours you wish to "work,"
- whether you want to be full-time or part-time,
- what size employer you want to work for,
- whether you want to freelance or start your own business,
- whether you want to work from home.

Today, more than ever, you can choose your own working hours. As discussed earlier, the driving force for all technological advances is based on the human penchant for finding easier and more efficient ways of doing things. That provides time for other activities (mostly intellectual and recreational pursuits) or for doing nothing at all—that is, to create leisure time. Why not for you?

Reduced Working Hours in the 21st Century

As mentioned, we are succeeding magnificently at putting ourselves out of work. We have reduced the number of hours devoted to human labour from 12-hours-a-day, 7-days-a-week (mostly on the land) to 7-hours-a-day, 5-days-a-week (mostly in the office).

Every technological revolution in human history has reduced the number of hours during which human beings are required to work, whether the labour be physical or mental. For example, ongoing automation in the textile industry has cut human labour input to a mere 0.1% of what it was 200 years ago.

The latest technological revolution has yet to have a significant effect on working hours. Although computers have handled an increasing volume or work without the need for more humans, the reduction in working hours since 1970 has been modest. Work was not shared and unemployment increased to levels unknown since the Great Depression of the 1930s.

Canada simply failed to adjust to the creation of the leisure society spurred by the latest wave of technological change. Coming out of the "Mini-Depression" with a so-called "jobless recovery" will force the government to cut the standard workweek to 30-hours by the year 2000 for a full-time job.

Flex-Time Jobs Grow in Popularity

More and more Canadians place a higher value on non-working hours. Many are even willing to forgo benefit packages and accept lower wages if they can have more time for themselves.

The desire to work less is reflected in the massive shift towards part-time employment, which is making a mockery of the traditional workweek. The number of part-time employees has increased significantly, from 12% of all jobs in 1973 to 26% in 1989. Projections show that 35% of work in Canada will be performed by part-time workers by the year 2000.

The shift to part-time work reflects the electronic revolution, changing lifestyles, and socio-economic values. Part-time workers and work-sharing improve the efficiency and productivity of the economy because two fresh minds are better than one tired one. And part-time work creates the opportunity for re-education and retraining as the work environment continues to change.

Part-time work thus becomes more and more embedded in our economy. What is happening is simple: part-time work is both convenient and attractive to both employee and employer. The key word is "flexibility," the business buzzword of a changing marketplace.

Traditionally, of course, part-time work has usually been lower paying and less secure, offering fewer benefits and chances for promotion. Fringe benefits and pension plans frequently are not available. However, a majority of companies now offer part-time work with pro-rated benefits, and almost 70% offer flexible working hours.

Telecommuting Becoming Widespread

Increasing numbers of Canadians are inventing new ways of living and working—with their families, at home. By 1993, more than 3-million of us (more than 25% of the labour force) worked at home at least part of the time.

As the PC and FAX join phone-answering machines to become the new standard in most homes, these work-at-home trends will accelerate. By the year 2000, up to 40% of us will be telecommuters. Of course, working at home demands self-management skills and you must be able to socially integrate with the "total workplace" and/or family or local community.

More and more people find they have no other place to go but into business for themselves. Entrepreneurship has blossomed during recent years of corporate downsizing. The number of sole proprietors has grown 23% since 1985, and most of them work at home.

Inventing Your Own Career

After considering the foregoing career factors, you now know much more about yourself and the kind of occupation most suitable for you. You've also thought about the future of your own life.

Now its time to "fix" your own future career by filling out the summary worksheet opposite.

After you've done that, the final step is to review your knowledge and skills and make sure you are properly educated, now and in the future, for the career you most want to pursue.

That's the topic of Section E, next.

SUMMARY WORKSHEET for INVENTING Your CAREER

(A) My Basic Personality/Career Match

Personality Type(s):	Potential Matching Career(s):
Most Suitable Field:	Most Suitable Job Function:

Preferred Work Pattern(s):

(B) Criteria by Which I Will Choose a Job Offer

Goals of organization I want to work with:

Types of people I want to work with:

Preferred working conditions/environment/location:

Types of rewards I would prefer:

(C) Preferred Skills I Can Offer

(i) Possess Now	(ii) Need to Acquire
In dealing with people: (i)	(ii)
In using technology: (i)	(ii)
In working with information: (i)	(ii)
Favourite/special knowledge: (i)	(ii)

Section E

Lifelong Learning
for Career Success

Don't you deserve one of the best jobs in Canada? Do you want to earn 50% or 100% more than your neighbour? You can have both—provided you get a good education and keep updating that education.

Education enables you to do what you have never done before. It gives you a distinct career edge. After all, what you learn is something that no one can take away from you. Expanded abilities and knowledge also hold the key to your future economic well-being. Indeed, more companies are tying pay increases to the mastery of new tasks. By spending 2 years to learn new skills, you can boost your income by 20% or more.

Today, then, a good education is more important than ever. About 40% of job openings through 2005 will require at least a 4-Year University degree, and at least a High School Diploma will be essential for the other 60%.

Those who drop out of High School will relegate themselves to boring and poorly-paying jobs. Don't gamble with your future. There is no substitute for education. Stay in school!

Higher Levels of Education Essential
Virtually gone is the time when a High School Diploma was all that was required to get a job that would last you for a lifetime. Only four of the 90 "best jobs" listed earlier do not require a High School Diploma. For vocational jobs, a High School "Diploma plus" will be essential for all but the least demanding (and lowest paid) positions.

Diplomas, of course, are like rare postage stamps. The more of them you "print," the less valuable they become. And even if you have a High School Diploma, the continued influx of immigrants increases the competition for the unskilled as well as the best jobs. An undergraduate University Degree or Community College Diploma is becoming commonplace. To-day, that extra education guarantees 50%-100% higher income. Without such qualifications, the best jobs simply will not be available to you in the late-1990s and beyond. As the following table shows, more and higher skills are needed in about every job, from floor sweeper to top executive.

Schooling Required	% of Jobs Requiring		
	1985	1995	2005
8 years or less	6%	3%	2%
Some High School	12	8	6
High School Diploma	40	28	20
Some College	20	22	18
College/University	15	24	32
Advanced Degree	7	15	22

While the economy is growing, the supply of graduates in some fields may continue to exceed demand until about 1997. In spite of rapid expansion in the professional and technical groups of occupations, there now is a surplus of labour which has to be worked into the system.

As we move into the late-1990s, however, an increasing percentage of jobs will require higher and higher levels of education. More than 60% of the new jobs created between 1995 and the year 2005 will need five or more years of train-ing/education beyond High School.

Because most of the best future jobs are knowledge-based, a Community College Diploma will be necessary in most cases. Of course, the best jobs will go to those with Masters Degrees and PhDs.

Taking Lifelong Learning for Granted

Re-education and lifelong learning are also future realities—at least until 2010 or so; and even then it is far from certain that today's knowledge explosion will have abated. At the rate at which knowledge is growing, it is estimated that by the time today's newborn child graduates from college, the amount of available knowledge will be five times as great as today. When that child reaches the age of 50 (in the 2040s) the amount of available knowledge will be 40 times as great as today. In other words, 98% of everything which is "known" will have been learned since today. Conversely, today's knowledge will account for only 2% of all knowledge in 50 years time!

In the future, therefore, university degrees will expire automatically just like driving licenses. And they will only be renewed after the degree-holder's abilities are checked. The rapid increase in new knowledge creates a need for continuous updating of professional skills. Investment in continually improving yourself through schooling, work skills and work experience is the best possible way to ensure your future personal satisfaction.

Gaining a Futuristic Education: "New" Basics

Let's be honest, you cannot wait for educators to improve the curriculum to provide an education that is constantly geared to a changing future. Above all, your education should emphasize "learning to learn," so you can find your way through ever more complex mazes of information. There is simply too much to learn. Instead, you need to know where to find knowledge (*not* to know it "off by heart"), to learn to sort out good (valuable, relevant, up-to-date) information from poor information, and to learn to manage and apply knowledge in long-term planning and decision-making.

Hence, your main educational goal must be to develop an ability to adapt as quickly and easily as possible to a constantly changing world. You must become a "learner" (not a student) and education must become a matter of learning to learn.

Those who do not learn will become the peasants of the Information Age.

The core curriculum hasn't changed for years. The "back to basics" movement, if carried out, will condemn young Canadians to backwardness. You cannot simplistically go back to old basics. Instead you need to ask: "What do I need to learn to be productive in 2050?" In sum, you need "future basics."

Future basics will include some of the old basics but much of the old content and way of teaching must change. We are living in a different world and education must change with the times. Future basics must include:

- **Social skills**, especially family studies, multicultural studies, communications/human relations skills of all kinds, negotiating skills, and a capacity for self-analysis and identity;
- **Technological skills**, especially the ability to understand the capability of modern technology, to be able to function with computers (but not to program them);
- **Economic skills**, especially information synthesis and management, economic management, generalist skills and the management of change in general; and
- **Political skills**, especially civic education about important social issues, goals and purposes, costs and benefits, and the ethics of citizenship.

Every career aspirant must have these new basics in their tool kit. Only by understanding the future will you lose your fear of it. And only by learning to think creatively will you turn society's challenges into career opportunities. I urge you to seek out those educational institutions that provide new skills and new ways of learning.

Computerized Education Speeds Up Learning
I also urge you to use computer learning systems. The Industrial Age spawned the still prevalent mass-production classroom

model of education—factories of learning. Today's students are hungry for information relevant to the future.

Mass education with rote learning bores them to death and drives them to frustration, if not right out of the system. While boredom is not the only reason, all studies show it to be predominant. In Toronto, 32% of students drop out before they reach Grade 12. It is much the same across Canada.

Instead, many watch television which, quite frankly, is far more entertaining. Even those who stay in High School watch an average of 28 hours of TV a week—about the same amount of time spent in the classroom—and only 4 hours doing homework. Such behaviour is a recipe for career failure.

Switch on the PC (not the TV)
If your school time is boring, at least go home and turn on your PC, not the TV. The computer is the ideal tool for individualized learning: you can learn at your own speed, review material, synthesize information and get feedback. There now is exciting software that moves beyond multiple-choice drill and practice routines to offer training in a variety of skills or advice of a tutorial nature.

Computers also break the time barriers marked by the ringing of the school bell, allowing 24-hour access to learning. You can thus learn according to your own biological clock. If you are a morning person, switch on the PC at breakfast time; if you're an evening person, turn to it on at night.

This is the future of education. Students of the future will "telecommute" into databases. These database "schools" will attract millions of learners who will have access to the best in education at minimal cost. Ultimately, the computer will have the capacity to reach every Canadian and provide better access to up-to-date knowledge that will enrich their lives.

I encourage you to fight for computerized education and to get your own in-home PC that will allow you to constantly update your skills in the pursuit of your chosen career.

Other Essential Career Skills for the 21st Century
Living with the future is somewhat like sleeping with an elephant. It can roll over on you. As we've seen, however, knowledge of future trends helps you to make a move "before the
elephant rolls over."

Mobility and flexibility are an increasingly important aid in
coping with shifts in the workplace. You need to be prepared
to move both mentally—from one field to another—as well as
physically, from company to company and from one part of the
country (world!) to another.

Agility and resourcefulness also requires generalist skills of
all kinds. Let's briefly review some of them.

● **People Skills**
All jobs require good people skills, whether in serving customers efficiently and pleasantly or so that employer-employee
contacts function smoothly. With the gradual erosion of sexual
stereotyping in jobs and in society at large, you also must be
comfortable in working with the people of the opposite sex as
equals, learning from work colleagues and supporting each
other in the task at hand. The same applies to working with
people of different cultures. Each culture has different ways of
doing things and we can learn much from each other. People
are people, just like you, and you must treat them as equals if
you want to progress in your career and in life.

● **Communication Skills**
If you can't communicate, you can't have a successful career.
Jobs are generally becoming more complex and require high
literacy skills. You not only need basic reading and writing
skills but the ability to organize and write fairly sizeable
explanations, instructions, letters, and reports.

● **Technological Literacy**
This skill has already been discussed, but it bears repeating.
Technology continues to change the way Canadians live and

work. Even in traditional jobs, workers must constantly keep pace with new developments and it is increasingly important to be able to work with computers.

Computer literacy does not mean that you need to know how to program a computer. It means having some familiarity with how computers work and being able to use their various software programs, whether in common office functions or in industries which use computer-controlled machinery and tools.

Anyone who knows how to use a computer to do their job more efficiently will have a distinct edge. For example, manufacturers and architects are ditching drafting tables and hand-drawn blueprints in favour of computer terminals that let them modify designs instantly. It thus also is necessary to continue to upgrade your computer knowledge as the technology advances so that you can develop new career path options.

● Commercial Skills
A knowledge of office systems and procedures is of importance to most jobs. Office equipment-use skills come in very handy in many areas: word-processing, spreadsheets, photocopying, faxing, computer operation, etc. Interpersonal skills also are needed by people directly involved in sales jobs as well as by those in other jobs, such as teaching or management.

● Positive Attitude
Your personal attitude will often be the *most* crucial in obtaining or retaining work. Attitude relates to such aspects as being willing to work hard, team spirit, eager to learn, and being flexible in adapting to both an employer and job requirements.

Vocational Training
The best way to gain a experience in all these basic workplace skills is to enroll in "Co-op Ed" programs. They provide you with day-to-day skills in the real world. Similar experience can be gained through internship courses, summer jobs, part-time work, and by doing volunteer work in various settings.

Ontario's *School Workplace Apprenticeship Program (SWAP)* is one of many such programs springing up across the country. *SWAP* allows you to learn a trade such as auto mechanics or carpentry while continuing to earn your High School credits.

Alternately, you may live within a few miles of one of Canada's community colleges which are the main centres of retraining. These colleges are very good at knowing about local job markets and many of them work with the local business community to tailor courses for specific skill needs.

According to the Ontario report *Making the Match Between University Graduates and Corporate Employers*, companies need employees who are creative and visionary. They must be able to manage change, understand the needs of customers and fellow employees, and be able to interact with them. In turn, 21st-century employees need a comprehensive skills inventory and a set of basic competencies *(see list opposite)*.

Career Trend-Tracking
To keep abreast of trends in your intended or chosen career, you need to read industry-specific or professional magazines and watch for company changes reported in the newspapers. Then you can take steps to upgrade your skills and so help make a job transition. For example:
- Radiologists might learn how to draw blood as hospitals consolidate diagnostic testing in one department;
- Accountants might take extra courses on the environment so they can assess environmental mishaps;
- Lawyers who learn about computer science or biology will be better able to apply patent and copyright law to software and biotech products.

Skills Inventory

- Problem Solving/Analytic
- Decision-Making
- Planning/Organizing
- Personal Organization
  & Time Management
- Risk-Taking
- Oral Communication
- Written Communication
- Listening

- Interpersonal Skills
- Conflict Management
- Leadership/Influence
- Coordinating Ability
- Creativity/Innovation
- Visioning
- Ability to Conceptualize
- Learning
- Technical Skills

Base Competencies

Innovating Change:
Conceptualizing as well as setting in motion ways of initiating and managing change that involve significant departures from the current mode.

Communicating:
Interacting effectively with people and groups to facilitate the gathering, integrating and conveying of information in many forms (e.g., verbal, written).

Managing People/Tasks:
Accomplishing the tasks at hand by planning, organizing, coordinating, and controlling both resources and people.

Managing Self:
Constantly developing practices and routines for maximizing one's ability to deal with uncertainty of an ever-changing environment.

(Source: *Making the Match*. Available for $20 from: Western Business School, University of Western Ontario, London, Ontario, N6A 3K7. Fax: (519) 661-3485)

Ability to Adapt Positively to Change

In our fast-paced world, adaptability clearly is a key skill. However, change is never easy for anyone to accomplish. If a change is a small one, people usually make the necessary adjustments. If the change is major, however, we often react with uncertainty, fear, disorientation, confusion, and loss of equilibrium as we try to adapt under pressure. But, as Confucius said, *"Only the supremely wise and abysmally ignorant do not change."*

All too often, however, the need to adjust develops during a crisis, such as losing one's job or failing a course. Our first response to crisis is to deny the need to change and to distort the true nature of the crisis. Though we may sense the need to change, we tend to convince ourselves and others that it isn't really necessary, that the problem will pass—or that a new opportunity will come along of its own accord. When changes pour in, we often react in a knee-jerk way, showing our inability to cope in a world we see as unpredictable, confusing, contradictory and overwhelming.

Every change represents both danger *and* opportunity. The best response is a positive one: to recognize and grasp the opportunities presented by change. For example, try to realize that a change in your workplace situation probably reflects a new world reality for your employer. With such a future-aware mindset, you can motivate yourselves to anticipate new career opportunities that stem from the change.

In today's world, the only constant is change itself, and there is no precedent for the many wide-ranging decisions faced daily by career planners. The 1990s are much different than the 1980s; the 21st century will be dramatically different. If you are to respond to instability and uncertainty, if you are to come to grips with changes and manage your future effectively, you must feel secure. The only constructive response is to understand the future and thereby feel at ease with change.

Conclusion

Envisioning Your Future Success

This book is my attempt not only to provide you with an antidote to future shock but to furnish you with a level of comfort about "what on earth is going on" and what to do about it. By understanding the forces of change and the career opportunities they present, you can be confident in your attempts to create your own future. By being in control of your career destiny through the taking of concerted action, you can also retain a true sense of identity and self-respect.

The world is in a historic period of transition. When you are in the eye of the storm, it is often difficult to see the direction the storm is heading and to appreciate its real dynamics. You must not let the storm overwhelm you. The present turmoil and confusion are quite natural under the circumstances.

Yet this huge storm of turmoil presents the greatest opportunity for career planning. You must understand what is happening and grasp the options presented by change. In such major upheavals, it is possible to achieve absolutely anything and everything. That's exciting. So let go of the past and grasp the future—your future!

Don't wait for success to come to you! Your future can be "managed" in a very literal sense if you recognize that you are in charge of your own destiny. None of us are without options. How you choose among the options open to you—and whether you create yet more new choices for yourself—will shape your future. You can begin to create the future you want simply by accepting that you have the power to do so.

But you must visualize clearly what you really want in life. Many of us shy away from thinking about what kind of future we want as opposed to what we expect. Creating a "vision" of your future potential thus is a very important step in the process of changing your life.

You must also become committed to that life vision. But don't be wedded to any one way of obtaining it. Keep your eye on the target. Focus more on your goals than about what path will actually lead to them. There may be many paths and the path you choose from time to time may turn out to be wrong. But if you are open to whatever paths might lead you to your goals, you are certain to achieve them.

Clearly, you must also learn what you need to know. In order to choose a path of action, you need information about what is happening in the world. While you don't need to know everything in order to act effectively, at least define what you must know and where that and other information can be found.

Apart from researching the library, asking questions is probably the most valuable part of collecting information. Become a "living question mark"—and continue to be one as you begin to take action. Be informed in as many ways, and from as many sides, as you can find.

Remember, there are no dumb questions. But as you begin to get answers, recognize that facts are often in the eye of the beholder, especially facts about what *can't* be done. You must be the final judge of what is reality.

Finally, choose a path of action and begin to follow it. Compare how things are right now with how you want them to be. Then define a series of steps that will begin to move you in the right direction. The steps should be easy and clear enough so that you can begin right now to do something that produces a measurable result, no matter how small, tomorrow, next week, or next month.

Set a definite timetable. And don't wait to know everything before getting started. You will learn much more after you take a few steps than by hesitating and trying to figure out which first step is exactly right. The important thing is to get started. Remember, there are three kinds of people in this world:

- Those that wait for the future to happen *to* them;

- Those that go out and make the future happen *for* them; and

- Those who are simply left to wonder *what* happened!

Decide *now* which one *you* want to be!

Your future literally is in your own hands. I dare you to be resolute. Move bravely into the future with bold and imaginative career initiatives that will ensure you grow and prosper.

Above all, remember that today's turmoil provides many of tomorrow's opportunities. Think about the future before you leap into a fixed career path and, whatever you decide, don't over-specialize in one restricted field. Success in the future will depend on the ability, as a generalist-specialist, to integrate ideas from diverse fields in order to create worthwhile futures.

Tomorrow really is the first day of the rest of your life. Your future career is waiting for you—inside your imagination.

Good luck!

Acknowledgments

I have been fortunate enough to invent my own career path. But none of it would have been possible without the help, guidance and encouragement along the way of a whole host of colleagues.

I particularly wish to spotlight the invaluable encouragement of, and learning provided by, all those who realize that tomorrow's best careers are still being invented:

- Maurice Dodgson for being my first generalist role model at Martins Bank in the U.K.;
- Harold Burns for giving me my first job-change opportunity—in a new country—with Toronto-Dominion Bank;
- Derm Barrett for introducing me to "the future" and for being yet another role model as a consulting futurist and seminar leader;
- John Hilliker for letting me create a new job and grow with him at Canadian Imperial Bank of Commerce, learning his dynamic management style;
- Hazel Henderson for encouraging me to change careers entirely and take the plunge to start out on my own as a consulting futurist;
- Richard Clark, Chuck DeRidder, Pauline Price, Erika Rimkus, and dozens more for their initial confidence in my public speaking and consulting abilities;
- Lu Congmin and Liu Dongsheng for opening the door to new career opportunities in China and Liang Fengcen, Lin Min, and Zhang Baogen for opening that door wider;
- The Canadian Federation of Students Services, the Canadian Guidance and Counselling Association, the Ontario College Counsellors, the Career Information Resource Advisory Group and numerous school boards/districts, school/college

principals, colleges and universities for allowing me to share
my ideas on future careers by speaking at conferences of
their members, faculty and students;

- Ron Szymanski at the Leigh Bureau in Somerville, New Jersey, for promoting my public speaking career among wider
audiences across NAFTA and abroad;
- Jim Williamson and Nick Pitt at Warwick Publishing for
patiently teaching me the tricks of the trade as a new author;
and
- Alison and Joanne Feather, my own daughters, for constantly challenging me to help guide their career paths—and for
helping me succeed in my own.

Thank you all!

May 1994   Frank Feather

About the Author

Frank Feather, Canada's leading futurist, is president of Toronto-based Glocal Marketing. The firm publishes the *FUTURE CONSUMER Newsletter* for business managers.

Mr. Feather is author of *THE FUTURE CONSUMER: Predictable Developments in Personal Shopping and Customer-Centered Marketing on the Information Superhighway* and *G-FORCES: The 35 Global Forces Restructuring Our Future*. He also has written widely in various magazines and newspapers and used to write a weekly column on the future for *The Toronto Star*.

In the field of education, he has taught continuing education students at Sheridan College and graduate students at York University. He also is a Fellow of Norman Bethune College at York University and has served on various committees there.

Since 1980, Mr. Feather has given more than 800 speeches in Canada and abroad, including more than 200 "Future Talks" at educational conferences, Professional Development Days and Career Days across Canada and the United States.

More than 80,000 educators and students have been stimulated by his provocative speeches on the future of education and tomorrow's best careers.

"Future Talks"
with
FRANK FEATHER

Re-Inventing Canadian Education for the 21st Century

Massive waves of social, technical, economic and political change are literally re-inventing Canada. The challenge is to realign ourselves with the waves of change so as to take advantage of the huge opportunities for innovation which are presented to those who are alert.

Canadian education (at all levels) is seriously behind the times and has no choice but to re-invent itself also. The college graduates of 2010 are already attending school. As tomorrow's workforce, living in a new world, these young people require new knowledge and new skills. This learning will come from a revamped curriculum, delivered by a new infrastructure in an entirely new way.

This session explains Canada's future and outlines implications which no educator of tomorrow can afford to ignore.

Tomorrow's Best Canadian Careers

Canadian students are perplexed: they cannot find suitable jobs; they don't know which career path to choose; they don't understand why the job market is changing or how fast. They don't understand the future—their future.

Drawing on Frank Feather's *Canada's BEST CAREERS Guide*, this session explains clearly how and why future trends are restructuring Canada's job market. Using a vivid 35mm slide presentation, Mr.Feather outlines where the best career opportunities will be in terms of geographic areas of Canada, by industry sector, and by job/career family and specific job title.

Participants will also gain insights into the types of educational study and other skills that are required by various jobs, learning how to prepare for and get the best jobs through futuristic career planning.

"Exciting and thought provoking,
you made our conference successful
beyond our most optimistic hopes."
Elizabeth Crosthwaite,
Assistant Deputy Minister, Skills Training & Apprenticeship,
Saskatchewan Department of Education.

Keynote Speeches Tailored to Your Program Theme
Contact Frank Feather Direct:
Tel: (905) 841-8008; Fax: (905) 841-8009

How to Order

Bulk Copy Reprints of

SECTION D
Futuristic Career Planning
WORKSHEETS

Section D is a comprehensive career planning section with easy-to-follow worksheets. While individual students may make a single copy of this section for their personal use, multiple copying is not allowed.

For in-class use or project assignments, Section D is available in booklet form by bulk order. Guidance counsellors also will find the booklet a useful tool for their clients.

Mail the Pre-Paid Order Form to:
Glocal Marketing, P.O.Box 38, Aurora, Ontario, L4G 3H1
. . . .

> > PRE-PAID ORDER FORM < <

Canada's Best Careers Guide Career Planning Supplement:
Futuristic Career Planning Worksheets Booklet

Please send _____ copies @ $5/each (incl. GST and postage).
Amount of $_____ is enclosed (pay to "Glocal Marketing").

Name: . . . .

Organization: . . . .

Address: . . . .

. . . .
   (City/Town)   (Province)   (Postal Code)